# Who's Bringing Them Up?

# Television and child development: How to break the T.V. habit

### Martin Large

"To see a World in a Grain of Sand
And a Heaven in a Wild Flower,
Hold Infinity in the palm of your hand
And Eternity in an hour."

*William Blake.*

## HAWTHORN PRESS

First edition 1980
Copyright © Martin H.C. Large.
All Rights Reserved
Second edition 1990

Published by Hawthorn Press,
Bankfield House, 13 Wallbridge, Stroud, GL5 3JA, United Kingdom

Typeset in Plantin by Acūté, Stroud, Glos
Printed by Billing & Sons Ltd, Worcester

Acknowledgements

The Oompa-Loompa's advice on television is reproduced from
*Charlie and the Chocolate Factory* with the kind permission of Roald
Dahl.

Many thanks to all those who helped with the suggestions and
material – especially Judy Large, Faith Hall and Audrey E. McAllen.

This book is dedicated to Elizabeth Large who taught me to see with
the inward eye.

*British Library Cataloguing in Publication Data*

Large, Martin
Who's bringing them up? : how to break the T.V. habit
television and child development. – (Lifeways series).
1. Children. Development. Effects of television
I. Title II. Series
155.418

ISBN 1–86989–024–8

# Concerning Television

"Turning on the television set can turn off the process that transforms children into people." – Professor Urie Bronfenbrenner.[1]

"Television is sensory deprivation." – Jerry Mander.[2]

"Without our television, we would not be a family" – ten year old London schoolboy.

"The continuous trance-like fixation of the T.V. viewer is then not attention but distraction – a form akin to day–dreaming or time out" – Fred & Merrelyn Emery, Australian psychologists.

"The greatest danger from television is the addictive, time-consuming effect that prevents normal growth of play, speech, co-ordination and constructive pastime" – Dr Adrian Rogers, Exeter.[4]

"The big thing for me is the protection of the children during the period of vulnerability in their lives. I think children under five should not watch television at all". – Dorothy Cohen, American educationalist.

"Marcus won't stop watching – not even the news – unless you switch off the set. It gave him bad dreams, made him restless, nervy and irritable – he's better now we don't have one" – A Bristol mother.[7]

"Television is here to stay, but we should be more intelligent about it. We should talk with the child about what he sees, rather than letting him sit for hours in front of the set. Today, we let the child observe what is going on in the whole world on television before we are prepared to let him cross the street on his own." – Bruno Bettelheim.[8]

"I believe television is going to be the test of the modern world, and that in this new opportunity to see beyond the range of our vision – we shall discover either a new and unbearable disturbance of the general peace or a saving radiance in the sky. We shall stand or fall by television – of that I am quite sure." – E B White.[9]

"In its short life time, television has become the major stumbling block to literacy in America. For all its technological achievement, television's negative impact on children's reading habits — and therefore their thinking — is enormous." — Jim Trelease[10]

"But most rebellious of all is the attempt to control the media's access to one's children. There are, in fact, two ways to do this. The first is to limit the amount of exposure children have to media. The second is to monitor carefully what they *are* exposed to, and to provide them with a continuously running critique of the themes or values of the media's content. Both are very difficult to do and require a level of attention that most parents are not prepared to give to child rearing." — Neil Postman[11]

"There may come a time when it is considered as damaging for young children to watch television, as it is for them to have a bad diet, to drink alcohol, or to smoke" — Martin Large[12]

"The consensus amongst most of the research community is that violence on television does lead to aggressive behaviour by children and teenagers who watch the programmes.... In magnitude, television violence is strongly correlated with aggressive behaviour as any other behavioural variable. " —[13] David Pearl.

"Television is good for your kids" Dr Maire Messenger Davis.[14]

"Television train people for only being zombies" Dr Eric Peper.

"Its like a drug... it stops them acting as fast as they would. It doesn't change them but it's like having half their brain taken away. And when you stop using your brain, other consequences follow." Cedric Cullingford[15]

# Contents

### Part II

# Preface

## *Advice on Television*
## *by Roald Dahl*

The most important thing we've learned,
So far as children are concerned,
Is never, NEVER, *NEVER*, let
Them near your television set —
Or better still, just don't install
The idiotic thing at all.
In almost every house we've been,
We've watched them gaping at the screen.
They loll and slop and lounge about,
And stare until their eyes pop out.
(Last week in someone's place we saw
A dozen eyeballs on the floor.)
They sit and stare and stare and sit
Until they're hypnotized by it,
Until they're absolutely drunk
With all that shocking ghastly junk.
Oh yes, we know it keeps them still,
They don't climb out the window sill,
They never fight or kick or punch,
They leave you free to cook the lunch
And wash the dishes in the sink —
But did you ever stop to think,
To wonder just exactly what
This does to your beloved tot?
IT ROTS THE SENSES IN THE HEAD!
IT KILLS IMAGINATION DEAD!
IT CLOGS AND CLUTTERS UP THE MIND!
IT MAKES A CHILD SO DULL AND BLIND
HE CAN NO LONGER UNDERSTAND
A FANTASY, A FAIRYLAND!
HIS BRAIN BECOMES AS SOFT AS CHEESE!
HIS POWERS OF THINKING RUST AND FREEZE!
HE CANNOT THINK — HE ONLY SEES!

"All right!" you'll cry. "All right!" you'll say,
"But if we take the set away,
What shall we do to entertain
Our darling children! Please explain!"
We'll answer this be asking you,
"What used the darling ones to do?
How used they keep themselves contented
Before this monster was invented?"
Have you forgotten? Don't you know?
We'll say it very loud and slow:
THEY...USED...TO...READ! They'd READ and READ,
AND READ and READ, and then proceed
To READ, some more. Great Scott! Gadzooks!
One half their lives was reading books!
The nursery shelves held books galore!
Books cluttered up the nursery floor!
And in the bedroom, by the bed,
More books were waiting to be read!
Such wondrous, fine fantastic tales
Of dragons, gypsies, queens, and whales
And treasure isles, and distant shores
Where smugglers rowed with muffled oars,
And pirates wearing purple pants,
And sailing ships and elephants,
And cannibals crouching round the pot,
Stirring away at something hot....
Oh, books, what books they used to know,
Those children living long ago!
So please, oh please, we beg, we pray,
Go throw your T.V. set away,
And in its place you can install
A lovely bookshelf on the wall.
Then fill the shelves with lots of books,
Ignoring all the dirty looks,
The screams and yells, the bites and kicks,
And children hitting you with sticks —
Fear not, because we promise you
That, in about a week or two
Of having nothing else to do,
They'll now begin to feel the need

Of having something good to read.
And once they start — oh boy, oh boy!
You watch the slowly growing joy
That fills their hearts.
They'll grow so keen
They'll wonder what they'd ever seen
In that ridiculous machine,
That nauseating, foul, unclean,
Repulsive television screen!
And later, each and every kid
Will love you more for what you did.

# Foreword
## *The Great Time Robbery*

Who is bringing up children? This question was prompted by the average twenty hours a week children spend watching T.V. This is more time than on other leisure activities, more time than school — and could constitute several working years by the age of eighteen. Viewing on such a scale is a 'great time robbery'. Such heavy viewing figures also prompt the questions of what effects television has on children, and whether this is what we want for our children.

A bleak picture of children and television was given by Cedric Cullingford's research over six years into the television habits of five thousand children aged six to eleven! Some of his startling observations from the research included:

— Television leaves a legacy of indifference.
— Children learn almost nothing from television.
— The more they watch, the less they remember.
— There was 'almost unanimous indifference to children's programmes'
— "The very idea of trying to recall features of programmes they have seen seems rather odd to children... They do not expect them to provide anything memorable".
— Children liked advertisements the most and remembered them the best.
— Serious programmes like documentaries are strongly disliked.
— Older children are far too sophisticated to be manipulated by advertisements — by the age of twelve, only one in ten children believes what even favourite advertisements say about a product.
— Educational television is probably least successful of all in imparting attitudes or information.
— Fifty percent of eight year olds watch T.V. regularly after midnight and practically all eleven year olds do.
— There is little parental control on what and when their children watch.
— Children get used to not thinking — television makes them enjoy not using their minds. Programmes such as children's broadcasts, educational T.V. and documentaries are disliked because they make demands on viewers.
— Violence could come from boredom, not directly from viewing, but

because of T.V. induced indifference and listlessness.
– Television is easy, undemanding and their home lives are organised
  around it.
– 'It's a usable commodity and parents can show their kids how to use
  it properly. I don't think it teaches them information. It's a negative
  thing. You can turn it into something positive, but left to its own
  devices children allow it to be negative:'[1]

These bleak findings contrast sharply with those families who are
creative – exploring activities, taking part in sports, playing games,
storytelling, celebrating festivals and being together. More and more
families are waking up to such activities, often with television in a
limited role.

Dr Maire Messenger Davis, in *Television is good for your kids*, tries to
put the positive arguments for television as a response to such research
as Cullingford's, or the first edition of this book. She maintains that
the careful use of television under certain conditions can be beneficial.
I agree with her for older children. For example, we now have a
television which our older children occasionally watch and make good
use of – when they remember! However, I consider that television is
not good for babies, toddlers, infants and young children up to the age
when they can enjoy reading, can occupy themselves, for substantial
periods and have developing interests. This is a personal view –
everyone needs to make up their own minds.

The theme of this book is the effects of television on child development. The main focus is not on the question of '*What are the effects of
the contents of programmes on children?*' – such as the influence of
violent behaviour – but on the question: *What are the effects on
children of viewing, of the television medium itself, irrespective of the
programme content?*

The nature of television watching will be explored, in order to
describe how television addiction arises and how this modern 'Pied
Piper of Hamelin' exerts its magical hold over children. After looking
into the process of child development, the influence of television on
the growing senses, on the health, on the education, on the family life,
and the socialisation of children will be explored. Finally, suggestions
will be outlined about alternative ways of breaking the television habit.

I would like to underline at this early stage that this book is specifically
about the effects of *television viewing* on children. This question is
relatively new, and the research evidence put forward in this book has

been pieced together from many sources. These are complemented by the many personal experiences of teachers, parents and doctors which have been included. Whilst clearly a great deal more research needs to be done on this question, it is in the last analysis up to readers to decide for themselves, on the basis of their own judgement and experience, what they feel is appropriate for children. The aim of this book is to be thought provoking and to stimulate new ideas about the appropriate uses of television.

Before embarking on the first chapter, I would like to sketch a story by Michael Ende entitled *The Grey Gentlemen*, who once committed a time theft on a similar scale to that wrought today by excessive television watching: —

Once upon a time there was a girl called Momo, who lived happily in a vault in a ruined amphitheatre. The local people gave her clothes, fixed up her room and often brought her food — in return, their children loved to play with Momo, who had the gift of helping them to invent such exciting games and stories as they had never experienced before — just by being there. A stream of adults would visit her to talk over their problems, because whilst Momo said little, she listened so intently that they were able to find their own answers. With her friends Beppo the Sweeper, and Guido the storyteller, Momo was happy in her new life.

But a grey shadow began to permeate the city and people's lives. It was a cold, silent invasion of which no-one was conscious. Invisibly, the grey gentlemen, with their ashen grey faces, their bowler hats, their grey suits, their steel brief-cases and their small grey cigars — went about the city stealing people's time. The grey gentleman knew that time is the essence of life, and that life lives in the heart. Their aim was to steal as much human time as they could — so that they could slowly take over humanity.

A grey gentleman would introduce himself to a potential client, like Mr. Fusi the easy-going barber, as an agent of the 'Time Saving Bank'. Then, with a cunning calculation of how much time was lost in idle conversation, in eating, being friends, sleeping or in day-dreaming, the grey agent would show his victim how much of his life had been wasted — and how much more modern, progressive and profitable life would be if a great deal of time was saved. But the grey gentlemen's victims could not remember ever having had visit afterwards — they forgot completely. Mr Fusi, thought, cut people's hair more quickly, did not talk so much as before, stopped seeing his girl friend, sold his budgerigar and put his mother in an old people's home. He never had any time to spare, and although the days grew shorter and shorter this only spurred him on to save even more time.

Meanwhile, the grey gentlemen collected people's "saved time". The media continued their work by advertising new time-saving inventions which might 'one day' result in a good life. It became unfashionable to be silent to relax, to enjoy life, or do a good job slowly. The city was transformed by demolishing all the old houses, by building huge tower blocks and a grid of streets. The children felt miserable, because their time saving parents had all but forgotten them.

Momo's amphitheatre began to fill up with children — refugees from all over the city. They puzzled her, because they did not know how to play, they tended to quarrel and brought expensive toys like talking dolls, robots or tanks which were so perfectly complete that nothing was left to the imagination. However, they soon began to enjoy playing the old games, using any old boxes, pebbles, clothes or sticks in the process.

But one day, when a new boy was spoiling the other's games by insisting on playing his radio very loudly, he blurted out how fond his parents were of him, how they proved their love with all the pocket money they gave him, and how they couldn't help not having time for him.

He cried, and the others understood, because they too felt abandoned. Momo then sought out her old grown-up friends who never came to see her any more so busy were they. This drew her to the attention of a grey gentleman, because she was hindering his work. One day, she found 'Bibi, the perfect doll' who told her, 'I belong to you . . . Everyone envies you because I'm yours . . . I'd like some more things.' But Bibi was impossible to play with, so the grey gentleman appeared and tried to persuade Momo to play with his dolls, in return for leaving her friends to save time.

Momo was puzzled because when the grey gentleman spoke she could her nothing. She listened so intently that he eventually blurted out the Time Saving Bank's secrets in his real voice:—

We must remain unrecognised . . . No one must know that we exist, no one must discover what we are doing. We take good care to see that no one ever remembers us . . .for it's only as long as we go unrecognized that we can carry on our business . . . It's a dreary business, stealing people's time in hours or minutes or seconds . . . because all the time they save is lost as far as they are concerned . . . We seize it . . . we hoard it . . . we long for it. Oh, you humans don't know what time is worth! But we know, and we are sucking you dry . . . and we need more . . . and more and more . . . because there are more of us all the time . . . more and more . . .[2]

How Beppo saw this grey gentleman sentenced to having all his time withdrawn, and how Momo met 'Master Hora' and eventually released human time from the cold grey vaults of the Time Saving Bank – you may like to read for yourself, because I do not wish to spoil your enjoyment!

The author of *The Grey Gentlemen* ends by recounting how this story of Momo was told to him by a mysterious figure whilst on a train journey. This figure, both old and young, finished his story by saying: –

I have told you all this as if it had just happened. I might equally well have told it you as if it had still to happen. As far as I am concerned, there is no great difference.

Grey gentlemen apart, there is much more to television than its obvious role as a 'time thief'. How, then, has television viewing become such an issue, and why is even BBC Television worried that children are watching too much?

# Chapter One

## *Television under Fire*

*T.V. isn't just in the environment.*
*It is the environment." John Leonard.*
*Edward Barnes (BBC TV) Children watch too much television.[1]*

Television viewing is the background of many children's lives. Young children watch the most, followed by school age children — for whom viewing is the most important hobby. Teenagers tend to watch less television.

Recent 1987 B.B.C. figures show an average of 19 hours per week for children aged 4—15 years — and 25 hours per week for all age groups. The 1978 PYE Television survey found that average viewing for a child aged 7— 17 years was more than 25 hours a week.

Consider the sheer *displacement* by T.V. of other children's activities like playing. Consider the impact of the *content* of countless cartoons, commercials, news items, soap operas, film and sport on young minds. Consider also the impact of the TV medium itself, regardless of content. Network television programming is now on the defensive — viewing hours are declining. However, satellite TV, cable TV, video, games, and home computers are increasing rapidly. There are more than sixty-six U.S. television channels. In Britain, there is now Sky T.V. and there are twenty one channels to date. The 1988 Guardian Businessman of the Year said that, "Video literacy is in, literacy is out." There are now more video shops than bookshops in the U.S.A.

So the television medium has become a constant factor in children's lives since the 1950's whether as a screen for home computer games, as a "learning tool" in infants' school, the focus of the living room and as "background" in children's playrooms.

However many people believe that children watch too much television. They are taking a critical look at the effects of viewing on family life, on leisure and on children's growth. Often, the realisation of the sheer amount of time spent watching shocks families into changing their viewing habits.

In spite of the repeated assurances that T.V. viewing is "good for you", such families have a healthy instinct for what is good for their children. Several well known researchers have backed this critical look at television viewing. For example, David Elkind, a child development specialist from Tufts University describes "the hurried child". These hurried children are so overstimulated by the pace of modern life — and viewing is a major factor — that they become stressed, nervy, tense and "old too soon" Neil Postman of New York University recommends that for children to have a childhood at all, parents need first to limit the amount of exposure to the media and secondly to monitor carefully what they do watch.

Often, what concerned parents need is some assurance that television viewing needs careful control for the sake of their children. This is what Neil Postman calls the "monastery effect" — in other words, children are helped to *have* a childhood, and may develop in the all round ways that heavy viewers are denied.

Doctors have begun to point out the harmful effects of television. Dr. Devlin, in a booklet published by the British Medical Association, called *Your Good Health* claims that Britain's national sport is watching television. He writes:

> Statistics show that the leisure activity on which we spend by far the most time is gaping at the goggle box... Instead of a nation of doers we have become a nation of watchers. Most of us seldom do anything more energetic than switch from BBC to ITV, or vice versa.
>
> You could say, I suppose, that all this telly watching has made us better informed on all manner of things, including our health, though as a part-time television doctor I rather doubt it.
>
> But there is no doubt of the effect which this change from being doers has had on our national fitness. As a country, we are hopelessly out of condition. . . no wonder our national standard of health is so poor.[2]

Other doctors have written about television holding back children's development, on the possibility of the T.V. screen inducing hypnosis, and the Health Education Council published a booklet in autumn 1979 indicating that television may be damaging to physical and mental health.[3]

Teachers have been no less forthright in pointing out the effects of television watching. The Association of Assistant Mistresses believes that television has almost stopped the transmission of nursery rhymes between the generations — something the Black Death and the Industrial Revolution failed to do. Because of television, rhymes like 'One, two, buckle my shoe' — so important for basic literacy and numeracy in infants — are largely unknown to children entering school.

The comments of teachers that many children are too tired and touchy to work well in the first part of the morning are supported by the viewing figures. There is now, of course, breakfast viewing, or sets being switched on in bedrooms whilst people get up. No wonder one primary school teacher said to me that two thirds of his pupils came to school,"....tired with bags under their eyes, from late television watching." A head of a local secondary school wrote a letter to parents about how many pupils could not work adequately because of excessive and late hour viewing. He observed that they came to school 'jaded and unfit to concentrate on lessons.'

The response of many parents of school age children is to limit viewing. Some parents have helped found *Action for Children's Television* in the U.S.A. — which campaigns for better programme *content*. ACT often praises British children's programmes — now threatened by Government changes. However, some parents believe that T.V. viewing, *whatever the content*, is not healthy for young children. For example Mrs Faith Hall, a speech therapist, teacher and mother of three children, founded the Gloucester based TV Action group to help alert parents about the effects of viewing on youngsters.

After the publication of the *1978 PYE Report*, Faith Hall felt, 'she had to take some action' to publicise the harmful effects of television on children. This report found that, 'two children in every three are watching television between three and five hours a day (21—35 hours a week),' and that three quarters of British children say their parents exercise no control over the numbers of hours they spend watching television per day or week, though most parents (more than two in three) set a deadline at which their children must stop watching and go to bed.'

Whilst nearly half of the 11 — 14 years age group completed their home work before watching television, 10% did their homework 'while watching' and 20% did their homework between programmes. News and documentaries were amongst the least interesting programmes, and one in three children had dreams about programmes they viewed late at night.[4]

The survey was of 7—17 year olds and unfortunately excludes pre-school children, who watch more television. In the U.S., surveys show an average of 30 hours per week for the 7–17 year group and up to 54 hours a week for pre-schoolers.

Faith Hall, on encountering these blunt facts, began to write letters to newspapers pointing out that, whilst the choice of the *content of a programme* is a matter for parents to decide – the act of television watching regardless of content – has serious effects. Television watching, she maintains, encourages passivity, poor concentration, distortion in perception, hyperactivity, disturbances of sleep, a distortion of reality and poor linguistic development in young children. The very act of television watching is inimical to healthy child development, physical and psychological,' writes Faith Hall.[5]

Her campaign was helped by two books on television which have been published in the U.S.A., Marie Winn's *The Plug-In Drug* and Jerry Mander's *Four Arguments for the Elimination of Television*.[6] Both books aroused much public discussion of the issue, shifting the debate from that of programme content to the effects of television as a medium.

Marie Winn's *Plug-In Drug* deals with the question of television, children, the family and of television addiction in children. Faith Hall has taken up many of these ideas in her campaign, in particular the basic message of Winn that 'It's not what you watch' – but the act of television watching itself that has the most harmful effects on young children.

Jerry Mander, goes the whole hog in advocating the elimination of television altogether. Television is not reformable, it is not a 'neutral' technology, and it is so harmful to the environment, to the health and well-being of people and to democracy, that it should be got rid of. Having himself used television for advertising purposes, Mander writes that 'To speak of television as 'neutral' and therefore subject to change. . . is as absurd as speaking of the reform of a technology such as guns.'

His arguments are complex and far-reaching, but the main points are; that television co-opts knowledge by encouraging us to doubt our own experience until this is backed up by 'experts'; that American television is controlled by a few corporations, thereby limiting access to the rich and powerful; that in human terms it results in poor health, passivity, and in conditions favourable for a 1984 type of totalitarianism; and that only gross linear information, such as Oracle Ceefax, can be put over effectively.[7]

Since the content of U.S. television is by all accounts poor compared with British television, these books produced a proportionally larger impact. However, since the arguments on the effects of television watching regardless of content — are equally applicable here, I believe that the debate will go on. The aim of this book is to help parents make informed choices with their children.

The book arose from the responses to a leaflet I wrote for the TV Action Group. This leaflet, *Television and Child Development*, was originally requested by my doctor , who needed helpful literature for parents. Reviews of the leaflet appeared in several national newspapers. Thousands of letters were sent in response. The great majority of journalists were keen to give accurate coverage of the effects of viewing on young children, to suggest alternative activities, and even to run experiments with families giving up television.

Even though newspapers carried such headlines as, 'Is Your a Child a T.V. Junkie?,' "The Television Disease; 'a mum's bid to ban the box'," and, 'Warning — "watching the box can damage your health,"' — the questions were raised. Television became a live issue, reflecting some of the questions raised in the 1950's in the early days.

The question of television watching had also become a live issue with BBC T.V. Edward Barnes, then head of Children's Programmes, said that children watch far too much:

> The average of 20 hours a week, which is the present estimate, is far too much. But if television is being broadcast, most children will find a way of watching it. So if programmes are not made especially for children to stretch their imagination, to involve them and inform them about the world around them, they will end up watching nothing but the least demanding programmes, effortless viewing like *Wonder Woman* and *The Incredible Hulk*[8]

However, Mr Barnes is in a difficult position, since he must be aware of the costs to children's development of television watching, which can be weighed against what he considers to be the benefits of programme content. Aware that there is 'no way the T.V. is a substitute for meeting real people' or play, Mr Barnes told Faith Hall on *Woman's Hour* that BBC Children's Programmes had once put out a short programme entitled, 'Why don't you just switch off your television and go and do something less boring instead?'[9] Since it will be argued that television watching is harmful for young children, Mr Barnes' further comments will be referred to again.

Several television film makers have commented to me how carefully they allow the television to be used within their families. One producer said that their young children did not watch, and the older ones watched a few selected programmes. The reason was that the creative abilities needed, for example to make a film, were not developed by children 'just watching'.

With all the letters came the request for more information on television, as well as many observations, experiences and comments. With a few exceptions, the letters were positive about the campaign. Here are a few excerpts:

> "My work in the school health service has certainly confirmed the same impression. . ." – a doctor.
> "As a teacher of thirty years, I have watched with alarm children's decreasing powers of concentration, a failure due in part to hours of unselective T.V. viewing. To think that some children spend twice as much time in front of the box as in school. . ."
> "I wrote the article because of a passionate concern about the noxious effects of television, not just on children and babies, but on all of us. (I was a member of what must have been the first television generation, virtually suckled on it)." – a journalist
> "I am only eighteen, but the difference between people of my age and younger, more T.V. – oriented children is already quite apparent. The extent of T.V.'s influence, and the dubious value of its content, really does worry me." – teenage student
> "As the mother of a young child, and the possessor of a television set, however, I am now concerned that my son should not be harmed in any way."
> "For many years we did not have television. Now it has destroyed a happy home, and lessened the children's ability for listening and language development."[10]

Many people wrote of how the television campaign had helped them in confirming their doubts and their reasons for not having a set in the family. But there were dissenting voices, like five sixth formers from Evesham:

> Being seventeen years of age, we have all been brought up on television, and can safely say, educated by it in many ways. We do not regard ourselves as having 'retarded brains'. . . We

must also strongly disagree with television 'depriving children of play' seeing as most children relate to television as a reality and imitate it. . .[11]

Such experiences of viewing, and people's healthy feelings are important. Many disregard their feelings and defer to "expert authority". A problem here is that researchers are divided over the positive and negative effects of viewing, even after years of painstaking research. This book will present some of this research, to enable readers to become more aware of the impact of television, and to make their own choices.

One unique study of the impact of television was made in Canada by Tannis Macbeth Williams. Children living in comparable towns with no television ('Notel'), one channel ('Unitel') and many channels ('Multitel') were compared. Second grade children in Notel scored higher on reading tests than in the T.V. towns. Notel children scored higher on imagination and creativity. When television was introduced to Notel (previously shielded from television until the 1970's by mountains), the researchers found several behaviour changes over two years. Children's aggressive behaviour increased. Their beliefs about girls' and boys' behaviour become more stereotyped. The advent of television in Notel had a negative impact on the levels of participation in community activities – this effect was particularly marked for people over 56. The researchers found evidence that television may affect performance by adults of creative, problem-solving tasks.[12] Reading in Notel was displaced by television as the most important hobby.

This study of Notel is important, since it compares people who live in a pre-T.V. era, with those for whom T.V. has become the background environment. As a "natural experiment", in which researchers could take "before and after" surveys, Notel has advantages over laboratory experiments.

Such research was not available when the first edition of this book was written. It was the sort of information people writing in response to the articles on television were looking for. People also asked for alternative activities to T.V., suggestions about how to kick the T.V. habit, how to deal with schools which used T.V. as a child minder, and how to revive family life after T.V.

This book will therefore explore the nature of the television watching experience, together with an examination of television as a medium.

The process of child development, and the optimal conditions for this will be reviewed. Some social, psychological, educational and physiological effects of television watching on children will then be described. Then, the question of kicking the T.V. habit and of alternative activities will be addressed.

The method of presenting the argument will be as much through the 'live material' given by people in letters, and in interviews and in newspaper articles as by surveys, or research findings.

If this book encourages more people to follow Edward Barnes' excellent suggestion to switch off your T.V. set and go out and do something less boring instead, I shall consider it a success. The first step in this process is to consider the questions, 'What is it like to experience television as a medium? What are your observations of children (and yourself) watching television? Is television a drug?'

# Chapter Two

## Experiencing television: the plug-in drug

*What do you watch? — ten year old girl*

*The Medium is the massage — Marshall McLuhan*

The critics of television have hitherto concentrated on the improvement of the quality of the content of programmes, on pointing out the
effects of violence, of anti-social behaviour, and of the examples of
family life that are played out on the screen. In Britain, the National
Viewers' and Listeners' Association of Mrs Mary Whitehouse is
concerned with improving the moral standards exemplified by the
'box'. In America, a group called Action for Children's Television
(ACT) has arisen to encourage more discriminatory viewing, to help
parents use television constructively with their children, and to
campaign to improve the quality of children's programmes.

Researchers have studied *the effects of the content of programmes* for
many years — particularly the connection between violence portrayed
on television, and levels of violence in society. Some researchers, like
Tannis Williams studying Notel, found that viewing did accompany
increased anti-social behaviour, while other social scientists have
found this not to be the case in their research. These concerns will be
discussed in chapter eight, since parents always raise them when I give
talks.

However, programme content is in some ways a side-issue, distract-
ing one's attention from the crux of the problem which is the act of
television watching itself, regardless of the programme. Whether one
is watching *Kojak, Playschool, Coronation Street* or *Match of the Day*,
one is still watching. Television watching itself affects children's
development regardless of the programme content. These effects
include the influence of artificial light on children's eyes and growing
organisms, the effects on the senses and on brain development,
sleeplessness, headaches, bad dreams, perceptual disorders, poor
concentration, hyperactivity and nervous problems. There are the
effects on language development to be considered as well as the effect

on the imagination, on cognitive skills, on social skills, on relationships and on children's sense of reality.

Exactly how children are affected is only just beginning to be examined, and it is to Marie Winn's credit that she first put the question of what the effects of television watching are — regardless of content. In her words, 'It's not what they watch. . .'that is so important, but the process of watching itself.[2]

This point was well put by an eight year old friend called Dawn, who noticed on a visit to our home that there was no television set. 'What do you watch?' she gasped in amazement.

If television watching was limited to, say, half an hour a day, or a few choice programmes a week for school-age children, then the effects of television watching might not be so critical. But evidence shows that many children spend a whole 'waking' day a week watching, therefore the effects of prolonged viewing need serious study.

## How much do children watch television?

The 'average' U.S. high school graduate has spent 15,000 hours in front of the TV — and 11,000 hours in the classroom. Children in the UK, USA, Australia and Canada view for three hours per day. In Canada, children of 2—6yrs watch 20 hours a week, whilst those from 7—11yrs watch 22 hours. According to the BBC the average viewing figures in the UK were:[3]

|         | 1984  | 1985  | 1986  | 1987  |
|---------|-------|-------|-------|-------|
| 4—15    | 16.10 | 19.59 | 20.35 | 19.14 |
| 16—34   | 18.16 | 21.36 | 21.10 | 20.03 |
| 35—64   | 23.24 | 28.04 | 27.49 | 27.25 |
| 65+     | 29.50 | 36.35 | 37.41 | 8.01  |

The decline in viewing of children aged 4—15yrs to just under 20 hours per week is explained by the rise of video ownership — 38% of British households owned a video set in 1986, but 64% of households consisting of a couple with two children had the use of a VCR, and households had a home computer.

Figures for pre-school children in America show that children are the largest television audience — viewing for a larger slice of their day than other groups. Winn mentions figures of 34 hours for pre-school boys, and 32.44 hours for pre-school girls in 1971. Some U.S. surveys have found that pre-school children watch as much as 54 hours a week. Other surveys point to an average of 20–30 hours per week.

These figures show the time children are in front of a television – even though they may not be watching with undivided attention. Television, therefore, has become the background for many children – switched on whilst they are talking, playing, doing homework or even sleeping. This was one reason why the anthropologist Margaret Mead called the T.V. the 'second parent'.

So more than a third of pre-school children's daytime is spent in front of a television set. This is a huge change of environment from playing indoors or outdoors without any electronic "massage".

Many people have discussed the sheer time spent in front of the T.V. Edward de Bono, who is a researcher into lateral thinking and creativity, estimated that even though no T.V. is watched until the age of five, 'by the time he's twenty, the average youngster will have spent the equivalent of eight full working years watching television'.[4]

Apart from the question of the effects of programme content, de Bono asks what the effects of television viewing are on the brain, on passivity, on the will, on the levels of involvement and of achievement. Of crucial importance to de Bono is what children are not doing when watching. He says:–

There is also the undeniable fact that those eight working years spent watching television would otherwise have been spent doing other things (perhaps worse, perhaps better). On balance, does the amazing educational and exposure value of television, which can bring to the meanest home experiences otherwise reserved only for the super-rich, outweigh the harm?

The last question needs to be answered for pre-schoolers by parents observing and deciding on what is healthy for their children. Since viewing comes after sleeping in terms of time spent, and since according to Roger Fransecky, consultant and psychologist advising CBS, U.S. children have watched 5–8,000 hours of T.V. before entering kindergarten – this is a vital question.[5]

John Leonard's comment that *television is the environment*, is supported by these viewing figures. Since one parental task is creating a nurturing home a few try our experiment. Observe people – especially

young children – watching television. Here are some observations of
children watching television.

## Observing children watching television

To observe children watching television can be highly instructive
about what they are feeling, and informative about the effects of the
television experience. A nursery teacher and parent observed the
following instance:

> There was a two and a quarter year old child whose parents
> doted on her and wished for her only the best, as so many after
> all do. I happened to call there one afternoon in 1977 when I did
> not yet know them very well. The mother was making marma-
> lade in the kitchen and the little child was watching *Play School*
> which her mother had put on for her. I was taken to the T.V.
> room to be with the child until her mother had finished. There
> followed one of the saddest scenes I have yet witnessed. She
> stood in front of the television set with her nose to the glass
> literally touching it, as if trying to climb inside (perhaps to find
> the lady whose hands, but not face, she could see). After a
> couple of minutes she rushed into the kitchen, only to return
> again and glue her nose to the lass. This was repeated about
> three times, each time the mother sending her back to sit quietly
> in front of her programme, presumably to be out of the way of
> the marmalade, for which she had also refused my help. After
> the third time, I could not bear it any longer and somehow
> managed to turn it off without upsetting anyone.[6]

This description illustrates both the use of television as a childminder
and also the problems some toddlers have when left to themselves in
front of the set. Just as my two year old son once asked me. 'How does
the man get into the box?' – the little girl seemed to be trying to find
the lady in the television. This is similar to primitive people seeing a
film for the first time, and being worried about where the man went
when he went off the screen.

A grandmother observed her grandson just after his second birthday, watching television. The family was watching, *Some Mothers Do 'Ave 'Em*:

> It was depicting the 'hero' driving a car which when he reversed hung precariously with the back wheels almost over the edge of a cliff. There was no panic. . . The driver said to his wife, 'Betty, I don't want to upset you. . . but sit very still. . .

> My little grandson, then not more than 2 years 3 months, threw himself face down on a large cushion crying out, 'No more car. . . No more car!' The set was switched off, and when it was soon after switched on again he protested 'no more car'. . . I remarked to his parents that I didn't think watching T.V. was good for him, as the boy was having extremely disturbed nights, which had been going on from about eighteen months old. . .

> The morning after this occurred, my grandson came to me with a little toy car, and balancing it near the edge of the breakfast table said 'Look – happen Nana' – Happen'. I was very troubled by this as it was obvious that he related the T.V. picture to his little toy car – without the appreciation that the T.V. was 'only pretending'.

Such observations of two year olds show what difficulties television watching may cause children at a time when they are learning to speak, to think, to find a sense of identity, and to discover the 'real world'. An adult may watch and know the car incident is 'just pretending', but do young children? Is the 'sense of reality' not something that develops in children over many years?

Another mother described a friend's two year old sitting watching television:–

> He wasn't really watching, he was just sitting there with a glazed expression, as if mesmerized by it. He didn't know what was going on, but only watched it because something was moving – the flickering motion attracted him, and he was put in front of the box to stop him pestering his mother.

The boy became hyperactive and woke a great deal at night.

The same mother relates how her fourteen month old daughter, in the rare times when the television was on, was always, 'Caught by the movement on the screen, even when absorbed in play she would turn round, attracted by a movement, sound or change of focus. . . Once when it was on at lunch, she just kept staring at it for ten minutes until it was switched off, even though she didn't understand what was happening on the programme. She'll play and ignore the television if it's a stationary programme!'

The above observations prompt the questions of *how* young children experience the high-paced T.V. medium − for example the average shot lasts for three and a half seconds, and there may be up to 1,500 different images shown per hour. It is a 'peek-a-boo' world − now you see it, now you don't.

In people's observations of young children watching television, many similar things were said. Even though the programme might have been much too difficult, or impossible to understand, such as the *News* the toddlers seemed drawn to watching like moths around a candle flame. However, if there was only talking and little movement on the screen (like *Jackanory* in which an adult tells a straight story), the children's attention might soon wander back to their play. Given movement on the screen, and stimulating events such as advertisements or cartoons, the children would once again become 'glued to the screen', 'attracted back to the television as though by magnetism', 'riveted on the box' or be drawn 'as if hypnotised by the programme'.

Now we have two parents describing their five and eight year-olds playing in their sitting room, where the television is usually on. First Jim, the father, who works as a T-shirt salesman and chestnut roaster, stated: −

We're the tele-addicts, not our children, they aren't T.V. zombies, just watching, but we are! The children will play, or Johnny will read, and will only sit still to watch the fighting bits, the shootings, the car chases and that, − they only like the exciting bits. Eight year old Johnny never sat down to watch a whole programme without fidgeting, even though he'll sit through a story told by his mum. They'll stop playing when the ads come on, which they like more than the films. Anything with a nice 'ding' to them![6]

The adults in this family are heavy viewers, as are the children, though for much of the time the television will be 'on' without them actually watching it. This seems to be so for many families; playing. visiting, eating and talking will happen in front of the television. Children in such environments seemed to be more 'hardened', 'and shut off' in order to do things, though their play would be intermittently interrupted by 'highlighted events' on the screen. The divided attention of young children, between their play and the screen in the background, may have an effect on the nerves, restlessness, fidgets, 'overactive brains' and difficulties in sleeping which many parents have reported.

A remedial teacher reported an example of divided attention in a child: —

> I was an observer in the lesson of a boy of 9 years. He was asked to draw the form of a very large figure of eight with one hand and a straight line with another, and keep them in constant movement on the sheet of paper in front of him. He did this quite well and then I noticed how he kept looking up and staring straight ahead with a blank look in the eyes. I realised that this was a habit and asked the teacher if he was a T.V. watcher. I was told that he was a heavy viewer.

Children who watch one hour a day, or less, seemed on the whole to be more sensitive to television watching. They were either not hardened enough, or had not developed a shut down mechanism — like the one Underground commuters develop.

Ellen, a mother of two, living in a small flat, described her children of four and seven in front of the television: —

> They didn't appear to be interested, just looking, just watching the screen, a one-way communication. They had little interest in the programmes, but at the same time they were glued to it. I noticed it made them quite nervous, and irritable if a programme was interrupted. If they watch before they go to bed, it makes them restless, especially *Star Trek* which makes them quite excited and stimulated![7]

One family with three children only seldom watched their lodger's set. The five year old boy likes *Playschool* and *Mr Men*; 'but is easily frightened by any sort of fierce character from Basil Brush up. He never asks for us to get T.V. and is quite happy never to watch. When he does watch he is absorbed totally and takes in the visual and aural aspects very strongly'.

This family's twelve year old boy, whilst liking many programmes, is often so involved and totally absorbed that he shakes in response to actions shown on the screen. His father says that:—

> Once or twice, when he has seen such a programme (i.e. science fiction or adult adventure films), he has been unable to sleep and breathes heavily with fear because of the recurring images.

This same family fostered an eleven year old boy who had hitherto watched television a great deal in a children's home. Interesting comparisons were made between the two boys' reactions — The father continues:—

> I sometimes would watch a film with him and in contrast to our eldest boy he would seem totally unmoved by whatever was happening, but at the same time would sit totally absorbed by the picture.[7]

It would seem, therefore, from such comparisons between light viewers and heavy, habitual viewers that they each respond in different ways. Just as a small amount of alcohol may have no effect on a regular drinker, whilst getting a teetotaller tipsy, so a small amount of viewing may result in sensitive emotional, sensory, physical effects in light viewers, whilst leaving hardened viewers untouched.

A mother of four described the television habits of her eight year old son, Adrian:—

> In winter, he comes home from school, switches on the television to relax, sits quiet and passively curled up in an armchair. He'll jump up, turn it off at the end of the children's programmes, rush out of the door, and tear around the garden on his bicycle.

Many parents commented that television seemed to 'relax', 'quieten', 'pacify', 'unwind' their children but after watching, they might be 'fidgety', 'nervous', 'bolshy', and 'unco-operative' as if coming-to after a bad dream. Marie Winn characterises this as a 're-entry process' from the changed state of consciousness experienced whilst viewing, back into waking, day consciousness. But what kind of 'relaxing' experience for children is television, if such withdrawal symptoms are so widespread?

Peter, the thirteen year old brother of Adrian, would 'watch television until it ran out' if he was left to himself. His mother spoke of: –

> The oppression the children get from watching television. They have open minds and seem sensitive to all kinds of impressions, for example the repetitive phrases and Kung Fu movements Peter picks up. If he watches for a long time, he'll just look like Dumbo for the rest of the evening, with square eyes that are red, quite pickeyed looking, he'll be aggressive as if foiled in watching and opposed to what the rest of the family want to do. Sometimes he seems mesmerised by it constantly coming at him.

Time and again, in describing their children watching television, parents I interviewed used the words 'zombie-like', 'passive', 'stupefied', 'mesmerised', 'totally absorbed but not interested', 'tranquillised', 'hypnotised' to describe their state. The exceptions were children watching short programmes with their parents, or children in homes where television was on all the time who had become hardened to the constant massage of the medium. After watching, there seemed to be widespread symptoms of edginess, nerves, clumsiness and outbursts of repressed energy.

What, then, do young children actually experience when watching television? What lies behind the glazed expression? Are they in a dreaming or waking state? One answer may be from the advertisers research into the 'T.V. – Brain phenomenon' – in short, the T.V. medium switches off the rational, decision-making part of the brain. The images can then enter a mind in a half awake, semi-conscious state. This theory of electronic massage will be discussed in chapter three. It could explain the "T.V. zombie" observation of many parents.

You could also ask yourself how *you* experience television watching?

## Adults' Television Experiences

Although I myself seldom watch television, when I do, it is easy to become caught up in the pictures, particularly when tired. It is difficult to keep my eyes off the screen – they seem to get caught by movements that compel my attention. Watching for more than a few minutes tends to make me restless, and it is an effort to sit still. Afterwards, I feel dulled with a lack of vitality, as though I need to have some exercise to feel 'together' again. If I watch in the evenings, images tend to remain fixed in my mind, far more vividly than my ordinary experiences of the day. At bedtime, try as I may to remove these images whilst looking back on certain people and events encountered during the day, they tend to return again and again.

Many people remarked on the relaxing, entertaining and informative effects of television on them. Others, whilst positive about the entertainment and educational value of limited watching for themselves, made these comments during interviews about television: —

> I just can't helping watching — it hypnotizes me.
> The mindless vacancy I get from watching T.V...
> Watching oppresses me.
> We're tele—addicts in our family.
> The children aren't hooked on T.V., but we are.
> Our family is glued to the television.
> It's like a drug you get lost in the euphoria.
> The more you watch, the more apathetic you get.
> Watching television drains me of energy.
> I was so vulnerable to T.V. watching, I had to get rid of the set altogether.
> It's like having an alien in the room.

Jerry Mander, who advocates the total elimination of television, describes his experiences as follows: —

> My reactions to the experience invariably reduced to one or two constants. Even if the programme I'd been watching had been of some particular interest, the experience felt 'anti-life', as though I'd been drained in some way, or I'd been used. I came away feeling a kind of internal deadening, as if my whole physical being had gone dormant, the victim of a vague soft assault. The longer I watched, the worse I'd feel. Afterwards, there was nearly always the desire to go outdoors or go to sleep, to recover my strength and my feelings. Another thing. After watching television, I'd always be aware of a kind of glowing inside my **head: the images! They'd remain in there even after the set was**

off, like an after-taste. Against my will, I'd find them returning to my awareness hours later.[8]

Since these experiences are of a subjective kind, it might be helpful for readers to observe their own responses to television watching, and to exchange these with others. Because people so frequently describe television watching as an addiction, let us now look at the 'plug–in drug'.

## Television – 'The Plug-In Drug'.

A drug can be something that artificially helps people to experience the pleasure, heightened stimulation or 'highs' that ordinary existence does not offer them. It enables people to embark on a 'trip' away from ordinary reality that they cannot do without, even though there may be painful withdrawal symptoms at the end of the trip, when a return to reality is made. Physical health, emotional well-being, family life, work, savings – all these may be sacrificed in the pursuit of the more extreme forms of addiction like heroin or alcohol. Furthermore, such addicts need habitually to repeat their trips in order to keep going, even though this may be harmful for their lives.

There are the well-known physical drugs, such as caffeine, nicotine, valium or barbiturates. Less obvious are such 'psychological drugs' as an addiction to some eastern guru, for example. I once knew a person who sacrificed his family life, work and a great deal of money to travel to festivals to see his guru, to whom he seemed addicted. The television habit is probably one of the most widespread psychological drugs.

Marie Winn believes that television can become a 'plug-in drug', a serious form of addiction, because it fulfils the above conditions. Tele-addicts retreat from the 'real world' into a passive but pleasurable state, removed from the worries of everyday life. They are unable to control their viewing hours, leaving many other things undone which they 'ought' to be doing. Furthermore, since so many people describe themselves as tele-addicts, with a 'habit', it is therefore justifiable to regard television as the 'plug-in drug'.[9]

For light, discriminating viewers, television watching may not be a 'trip'. They are using it with detachment for purposes they find personally appropriate. Perhaps young children are not tele-addicts initially because they prefer to be actively involved in play. However, it is evidently very easy for children to become addicted as the following example illustrates. A nursery teacher wrote the following description:—

> The four year old son of a friend of mine watched regularly such programmes as *Playschool* and *Blue Peter*. His mother sensed that television watching was not healthy, but being of a weak will continued to let him see his programmes. He was subject to nightmares and night waking as well as aggression. These latter were surely also bound up with much over-stimulus of various kinds (ambitious parents, poor quality toys and books, etc.). One night he awoke and screamed that they should throw the television to the bottom of the garden. (It appeared that this was not merely a repetition of what someone had said.) Sadly, his parents did not take heed of their young son's desperate and still healthy cry, and now, at six, his mother has a physical fight with him to drag him away from the box.

The temptation for parents to allow their children to watch television is great, particularly at 'rush hour' times after school and before the evening meals. This may be enough to cause children to become tele-addicts, which in turn results in their being less able to play by themselves. They then may want to be amused by their hard-pressed parents who may take the easy option of giving another dose of the plug-in drug, thus completing the vicious circle.

I have observed many toddlers and infants who are so keen on playing with each other, that they forget about watching the programme. Playing 'doctors', 'trains', or 'shop' is much more involving. For example, a play therapist in a children's hospital remarked that:—

> If *life* itself is interesting and absorbing the child will lose interest in T.V. One child in hospital who was busy in our play group was called by his mother to watch *Playschool* on the hospital T.V. but the four year old said. 'No thanks, I am *in* Playschool'.

Since the natural desire of young children is to play, to be active, to explore, to engage in concrete activities — the act of television watching itself, of being a spectator, cuts right across children's needs to do things, to be in *Playschool*, not merely to watch it. As adults we have developed the ability to be spectators, separate from what is observed, thus many of us do not readily understand how different children are. They are active doers, not passive observers — which television watching may condition them to become prematurely.

A further observation about television addiction was made by several teachers, who remarked that pupils seemed less attentive on winter Mondays, after a large weekend dosage of television watching, than on the other school days. One teacher said that:—

> To achieve a good lesson on Monday morning I have to devote at least the first half an hour to movement in all its forms — P.E., imaginative movement, recitation of poems, singing, multiplication tables, etc. This is the only way to overcome the effects of the psychological drug imbibed from weekend T.V. watching.

The Monday morning T.V. syndrome was paralleled by the struggle teachers have at the beginning of term. Even though many children are by that time 'bored' by being at home, teachers remark that it may take several days, if not a fortnight, to develop an active, receptive, attentive and creative mood in their pupils.

The 'Monday morning' and 'first days of term' observations may be likened to the withdrawal symptoms shown by lighter viewers when they have just finished watching.

To conclude, television watching can be addictive, and often young children either fall into the habit or are educated by their parents into being hooked. But what is it in the nature of television that makes it addictive? Is television inherently addictive? Why is the screen so attractive that many children spend more time in front of it than with their parents or in school?

# Chapter Three

## *The Magic of the T.V. Pied Piper*

*We are not concerned with getting things across to people so much as getting things out of people. Electronic media are particularly effective tools in this regard because they provide us with direct access to people's minds — Tony Schwartz, The Responsive Chord.*[1]

In the pre-television era, playgrounds, streets and greens were alive with children playing a multitude of games and singing rhymes, sometimes unchanged for centuries, carrying out traditional customs and doing all the activities forming our 'children's culture' described so vividly in the Opies' *Language and Lore of Schoolchildren.*[2] Seasonal games like conkers or marbles, top spinning, hoops, skipping to rhymes, local customs such as 'mischief nights', jingles, hopscotch and countless other activities formed the rich fabric of children's culture. In the 1950's, a version of *Davy Crockett* took few days to get from a Cardiff playground to Newcastle upon Tyne. Weeks after Edwards VIII's abdication, children all over the country were singing 'Hark the Herald Angels Sing, Mrs Simpson's pinched our King!'. This age-old children's culture is semi-underground, and not for the usual adult.

Nowadays, although children's culture may still thrive on some school playgrounds in certain areas, one can be in a park or on a street at a time when it would once have been bubbling with children playing; now there are but few children, and even fewer who play the old games. Where have all the children gone on a Saturday morning, a Sunday afternoon or after school? The television, like the Pied Piper of Hamelin drawing all the children into the mountain cave, has taken many of our modern children away from their hobbies, play, games, streets and green for at least twenty hours a week. Only the few odd ones out who watch little or no television continue to play, to 'muck about' as we used to say in Yorkshire, as 'old-fashioned children'. This latter term is often used by some friends to describe our own children — who play vigorously, occupy themselves well, demand little attention — and who love a romp or a story.

How does the magic work? How are eyes glued to the tube?

## *Gluing eyes to the tube at an electronic pace*

Television 'images' are generated by electronic scanning. Countless small phospor dots, formed into 625 lines (525 in North America) are activated by a cathode ray gun scanner, which fires electrons along alternate lines. In one thirtieth of a second, the scanner sweeps twice across the screen to core the alternate lines of phosphors. The eye receives each dot, and this is transmitted to the brain. The brain then "fills in" the dots of each scanner pattern, below the level of our conscious awareness. The only image is the one we create in our brain – by linking up the required dots – a scatter of dots like a tea strainer or like a children's colouring book where lines have to be connected between dots.

The generation of illumined dots at thirty (or fifty) times per second puts a strain on the visual system, since the eye and conscious brain can only record visual stimuli at twenty impulses or less per second. The experience of 'not quite keeping up' with the electronic pace of the scanner may be a physical factor in gluing eyes to the tube. Another way of expressing this is the common experience of being in a room with a T.V. set on. Even though the programme content is of no interest, and one is doing something else, one's eyes often wander and "get caught" by the screen. The sight of babies is extremely sensitive to bright lights and visual over-stimulation. Yet many young babies are put near T.V. sets "to put them to sleep". This may be a stress reaction, since babies are completely open to their surroundings. Burton White, in *The First Three Years of Life* describes the baby in the first six weeks as:—

generally unusually sensitive. . . . It is perfectly normal for an infant to startle and cry at any abrupt change in stimulation during her first few weeks of life. Such common reactions include a response to sharp nearby noises, or to jolts to the crib or bassinet, or to any rather sudden change in position, particularly when the baby has been inactive. A second, less dramatic indication of sensitivity at this age is the infant's avoidance of bright lights. A Phase I infant [birth to six weeks,] will keep his eyes tightly shut in a brightly lit room or when outside in the sun. In fact, he's much more likely to open his eyes and keep them open in a dimly lit room than in one at an ordinary level of illumination.[3]

For toddlers and infants — whose sight is sensitive and developing, the powers of forming images out of dots may be stressful. The young viewer is absorbed into the powerful electronically stimulated medium.

## "Viewing is at the conscious level of somnambulism"

A second cause of "T.V. addiction" was put forward by Australian Researchers, Fred and Merrelyn Emery. They believe that the special kind of light T.V. sets give off closes down the mind. The human nervous system finds it hard to cope with the light because firstly it is 'radiant' and not 'ambient' light, and secondly because it is rapidly switching on and off.

Most objects we look at leave our eyes alone — they give off ambient, or reflected light. But if you look at a light source itself, you get radiant light at a high intensity. The Emery's say that,...'the human perceptual system evolved to deal with ambient light, not radiant light.' Evolution has not developed human sight for looking at radiant light so we don't try to do it. We cut off.

The second cause of the mind closing down, is the rapidly pulsating light — on and off fifty or sixty times per second. This rapid pulsation could produce 'habituation'— the brain gets used to the rate of light pulses, becomes fixated by them, so that the content of the programme is displaced.

The Emery's likened the television to a technological hypnotist, with the brain dominated by the signal. "Provided the viewers continue to watch, they are unlikely to reflect on what they are viewing."

The hypothesis that T.V. as a radiant repetitive light source — closes down the brain, may explain why many people describe themselves as 'mesmerised' or 'hypnotised' by the medium.

Observe people viewing — the 'television stare', the fixed position of the eyes and head, the minimal movement of the eyes — which take in the whole screen in a slightly de-focused way. By contrast in normal vision, the eyes are continually moving and focusing. As focused eyes are usually a sign of conscious attention, then the "Zombie — look" of viewers may be understood as indicating a hypnotised, semi-conscious or dreaming state in which the viewer is barely conscious. The Emery's believed that, 'viewing is at the conscious level of somnambulism.' In other words viewers are held barely awake by the medium.[4]

The Emery's based their findings on experiments which have totally shaken up the way in which T.V. is used for product and political advertising. It was discovered by accident how T.V. could give, "direct access to peoples' minds".[5]

## The T.V./Brain phenomenon

T.V. transmits, *"information not thought about at the time of exposure."* Herbert Krugman.[6]

Whilst the television may be on for long periods, people may only be watching intermittently. This is ideal for advertisers or those seeking attitude change via television. Tony Schwartz, who used T.V. "as a door to your home, even as a door to your mind" in the 1976 Carter election wrote in 1973:

> Recent attitude change has shown that the most favourable condition for affecting someone's attitude involves a source the listener depends on or believes in, and yet one he does not actively or critically attend.[7]

Herbert Krugman, later manager of public opinion research at General Electric H.Q., Connecticut, researched into the physiological responses of the brain to T.V. watching. Using electrodes from subjects' heads, he observed brainwave patterns on an electroencephalograph.

With repeated trials with T.V. viewers, within thirty seconds the brainwaves switched from beta waves — indicating alert and conscious attention — to alpha waves. These indicate an unfocused, receptive lack of attention — a condition of subconscious day dreaming and aimless wandering. Krugman was impressed at how quickly the alpha state emerged.

For readers of books and magazines, beta waves reappeared — a sign of alertness, attention and awake consciousness.

The basic methods of Krugman's experiments have been developed and the findings have been explained by various hypotheses, and then applied systematically.

Another U.S. experiment had ten children watching their favourite T.V. programme. Dr Eric Peper of San Francisco State University hypothesized beforehand that because the children were *interested,* brainwave patterns would alternate between beta and alpha waves, but, "They didn't do that. They just sat back. They stayed almost all the time in alpha. This means that while they were watching they were not reacting, not orienting, not focusing, just spaced out."[8]

One explanation of the T.V. brain wave patterns being similar to staring at a dark wall in a dark room with one's mind off or to sensory deprivation experiments, is that T.V. closes down the logical left brain, leaving the right hemisphere open to incoming images. The left hemisphere of the brain is concerned with sequential logic, words, analysis and reasoning. It processes only one stimulus at a time, leading to orderly sequences of thought. The left brain "tunes out" when viewing T.V. The right hemisphere is concerned with images, colours, rhythms, emotions – processing information emotionally and non-critically. The left brain takes in the *content* of what someone says, the right brain takes in the non-verbal gesture, tone of voice and gaze.

Whilst viewing, the non-critical right brain can work unhindered. Krugman wrote in his report:

> It appears that the mode of response to television is more or less constant and very different from the response to print. That is, the basic electrical response is clearly to the medium and not to content difference. [*Television is*]... *a communication medium that effortlessly transmits huge quantities of information not thought about at the time of exposure.*"[9]

The possibilities offered by a medium which offers direct access to people's minds have been developed in highly sophisticated ways in the 1980's. Television has become a powerful political and commercial tool, used in ever more subtle ways to persuade, influence, plant images and form minds.

For example, few commercials now spell out the logical reasons for buying product X – a left brain appeal. Commercials now make use of images, feelings, sounds and associations that are pleasant. These resonate with our deeper feelings, values, beliefs and expectations – which are associated with a product, service or political candidate when we face real life choices. We can remember Mrs Thatcher stroking a calf, serving behind a fish and chip counter, or driving a fork lift truck – but little of her policies. Long after the 1986 U.K. General Election, we can picture Neil and Glenys Kinnock on a headland overlooking the sea with a seagull soaring above them. One can remember Ronald Reagan's "sincere gaze" smile and "warmth" as conveyed on television – but little of the policies. These are all "right brain approaches" – all "presentation" and no substance.

The reason many people feel they cannot switch television off may be that the decision-making, analytical left brain has been tuned out. The Emery's consider that viewing decreases vigilance and preparedness for action : –

> The nature of the processes carried out in the left cortex and particularly area thirty nine (the common integrative centre) are those unique to human as opposed to other mammalian life. It is the centre of logic, logical human communication and analysis, integration of sensory components and memory, the basis of man's conscious, purposeful and time-free abilities and actions. It is the critical function of man that makes him distinctively human.

To conclude – the T.V./brain phenomenon could explain how some of the magic of the 'T.V. pied piper' works. The medium tunes out the logical left brain, and tunes in the uncritical right cortex which processes images 'not thought about at the time of exposure.' Not only is it hard to switch the set off, but the medium puts one into a semi-conscious/half dreaming state "spaced-out". Whilst in this state, one is powerless in one's mental household – and the images come in unfiltered.

## Resisting 'the basic electrical response of the brain to the medium.'

However, according to the findings of brain hemisphere research, it is possible to choose the mode of thinking with which we embrace an activity. Robert Ornstein, a leading researcher, suggests that the left and right brains are specialised for the kind of thinking people choose to use. This type of thinking need not be controlled by the medium they confront.

Therefore, T.V. viewers can watch analytically and critically – evaluating, judging, noting camera angles, editing sound-image links, frames, stereotypes opinions, bias. However, if one does this – for example by taking notes – one may experience being pulled from the analytical to the non-critical viewing state. This process of conscious viewing involves what Krugman calls "resistance" to the "basic electrical response of the brain to the medium".

Most viewing does not encourage conscious attention. We are tired, wish to relax and the effort of critical attention is not worth it. In any case, Marshall McLuhan maintained that the, "response to the medium may well be at the level of the nervous system, working its larger effect regardless of critical analysis on the part of the viewer."[10]

Media education may encourage critical viewing — but young children are far more vulnerable to T.V. than the adults in Krugman's studies. One conclusion from these researches is that most adults, let alone children, find it hard to prevent T.V. tuning them out.

## *Highlighted content to hold your attention.*

The aim of programme makers is to hold the attention of the target audience. This is a sophisticated art, since the T.V. medium itself is visually poor compared with film. One reason for the slightly blurred T.V. screen is the rapid illumination of dots — whereas with film, real images are projected at twenty four frames per second. Films can contain much visual subtlety and contrast. When films made for the cinema are then shown on television, much of the detail may be lost because the process of televising reduces complexity. T.V. producers have therefore to select images which are as clearly differentiated as possible from the background. T.V. plays, for example, are performed with the minimum of scenery, and close ups of peoples' faces are frequently made against plain backgrounds. Because of the lack of high quality sound and picture, producers tend to programme high-lighted content, such as violence, anger, competition, conflict, argu-ment — in other words, any images conveying an impact that will attract the viewer's attention. The more subtle feelings of love, tenderness, pity, compassion, empathy or caring have little visual impact. This is why sports programmes, conveying much action, westerns, crime series and even the news may make 'good television', because the technical limits of the medium cause such content to be the most attractive.

Jerry Mander describes television's fuzzy images as an inherent 'bias against subtlety' and towards 'the coarse, the bold and the obvious'.[11]

Even highlighted incidents are not sufficient to hold the viewer's attention for long, and therefore producers employ a battery of technical tricks aimed at riveting your mind to the set. Jerry Mander invented the 'Technical Events Test' for one to discover how many such eye-catching techniques are used.[12]

Next time you watch, count the number of cuts, zooms, shifts of focus, changes of pace in the music, superimpositions, words on the screen, voices over, speed ups, slow downs — that take place every minute. There are many other techniques to watch for. T.V. is two-dimensional, so images alternate between several cameras to give the impression of depth. Try counting the cuts. When there is a cut from the outside of a building to the inside, where a group of people are talking — how do you know it is in the same building? Look for visual cliche's, New York imaged by the Statue of Liberty, a press reporter reporting from outside the White House. Spot the stereotype and which disadvantaged group is portrayed. Catch the cutaway — all the editing, the shots of an interviewer's back or face that splice the bits of an interview.

The producer knows what the attention-span of the target audience is. This span may be a few seconds, half a minute or a minute. He has therefore to insert a technical event in order to re- awaken a waning interest to jolt you back to attention, and to drag you to the next stage of the story line.

I remember watching a documentary in which the main technical trick was a dark wedge slowly wiping the previous scene off the screen, accompanied by a loud grating rattle. It happened every minute or two.

Since the number of technical events determines the level of viewing, advertisements are packed with them to stop viewers taking a break. It was not therefore surprising to find how many children 'liked' watching commercials, particularly cartoons where many unusual things happen. The number of technical events, and the pace of images, rises at peak times in programmes. They are much less frequent in special interest programmes such as documentaries or 'talking heads'. The News and commercials, however, contain many technical events. In a sense, the News is like a series of commercials. How do T.V. producers know about peoples' attention span, and what technical events to use? The A.C.Nielsen Company has developed sophisticated surveys which give audience sizes, ratings, and responses to both programmes and commercials. These ratings determine advertising costs, for example NBC's *Miami Vice* could charge in autumn 1986, $165,000 for each thirty-second advertising slot. This programme attracted affluent male Yuppies.

Nielsens use audimeters to track the viewing habits of 1200 U.S. households — selected as a representative sample. These audimeters provide the data which T.V. ratings are computed from. The audimeter records the viewing of a household, T.V. channels, times, — and feeds the data to a central computer in Dunedin, Florida which produces ratings and shares of available viewers, socio-economic background for each programme. So detergent and food advertisers would prefer a $195,000 thirty second slot on *Dallas*, watched primarily by female viewers.

Nowadays both *purchasing and viewing* habits are monitored and connected — so the results of T.V. commercials can be assessed immediately by the level of sales. Everett Holmes, a vice president of Nielsen said: The joining together of these two measurements will enable marketeers to measure the entire sequence of consumer behaviour — from what people view to what they do.[13]

In Toronto, the sample of 2000 households used by Nielsen's have "people meters" which monitor all individuals, and electronic I.D. cards for supermarket purchases. Joyce Nelsen describes how the system works:—

Every three seconds, the people meter scans the tuning activity of the set and detects precisely which station is being watched and by whom, and it recognizes whether or not that station is being received off air, by cable, or via satellite dish. It also selects "Zapping" — the skipping of commercials through the use of the remote channel selector — and informs the advertiser which portion of the ad (if any) held the attention of which viewers. Of course, the same thing is true for the programmes : the people meter, scanning the TV set every three seconds, lets a programme maker know where a significant portion of viewers (and which ones demographically) zapped to another channel. The system also monitors individual use of VCRs, videogames, and personal computers hooked into the TV set. Every twenty four hours, during the wee hours of the night, all this information in each people meter is automatically transferred through the the phone lines to the central computer.[14]

This data is then correlated with the supermarket check out data supplied by the household I.D. card. Such data is used by programme and commercial makers as feedback — and if people are changing channels, zapping, or switching off, they attempt to keep the target audience's attention by inserting the appropriate technical event or image in subsequent programmes.

So the highly sophisticated methods used by T.V. programmers to hold the audience's attention by monitoring, "what they view and what they do," by using technical events and images — are other ways of exerting T.V. pied piper "magic".

*Sesame Street* is an example of how television producers keep children's attention, using techniques from the advertising world.

## Sesame Street: Geared to T.V. Addiction?

*Sesame Street* has been produced by the U.S. Children's Television Workshop in the U.S. for over ten years. It is aimed at pre-school children and according to sociologist Rose Goldsen is designed to glue them to the tube for the entire programme. Since it is marketed internationally, it constitutes a massive intervention into the traditional children's cultures of many countries.

To ensure maximum attention, each part of *Sesame Street* is tested on children with an accompanying 'distractor' machine. According to Marie Winn and Rose Goldsen the producers found by this means that cartoons and catchy stories had the most riveting effects — also what children's attention-spans were. Not surprisingly, *Sesame Street* concentrates on many of the techniques used to make commercials. Instead of selling Mrs. Thatcher like soap powder, the letter 'L' and the number '3' are sold using slick advertising techniques.

Joan Ganz Cooney, a founder of CTW, observed: —

An early conclusion of parents and experts who observed children's watching habits was the fact that children responded most positively to commercials. They learned to recognise words and phrases long before they actually learned to read because of the simple, direct methods of rhetoric employed in the one minute product commercial. Pace, style, jingles and repetition are key elements. At the workshop we intend to 'sell' — if you will — the letters of the alphabet and numbers... [15]

In other words, in order to sell nursery rhymes, words, letters, numbers — pre-school education — there are commercials, packaged and put over using all the techniques of television advertising that are necessary to guarantee attention.

Each programme of fifty four minutes is made up of thirty to forty parts, eight of which take place on Sesame Street. The other parts are cartoons, puppet episodes and bits of film that are interspersed with the Sesame Street happenings which make up the day's story. The programme is introduced by a figure, such as Gordon, introducing the letters and numbers starring that day.

Various technical events are used in quick succession in order to rivet letters into viewers' minds. For example, after Gordon holds up a billboard to plug the letter 'Y', the screen momentarily goes blank, then lights up, a cartoon yellow bird appears, then alights on a Y-shaped tree. A voice says, 'This is the Yellow Yahoo Bird...When you ask the Yellow Yahoo if he enjoyed this lunch he answers, 'Yes, quite Yummy', and then he Yawns'. At every 'Y', the screen registers the letter 'Y' which may elongate, contract, change colour, move around and perform in eye-catching ways. Such a sequence takes a minute, and employs many of the techniques used to make commercials – except the letter 'Y' is being sold and not deodorant.

How producers get children to watch *Sesame Street* is clear – it is a programme geared to T.V. addiction for pre-schoolers. Fortunately, the BBC has not chosen to rivet children's attention in such a way. Monica Sims of the BBC once said:

'We're not trying to tie children to the television screen. If they go away and play half-way through our programmes, that's fine'. [16]

## Conclusion: how the plug-in drug works.

Television is a powerful medium which adults, let alone children, find easy to become addicted to. One's eyes are glued to the tube by the fast electronic pace, a wealth of images and technical events; highlighted content is designed by programme makers to hold your attention; the T.V./brain hypothesis of Krugman suggests that the medium tunes out the critical left brain, putting us into a spaced out state open to whatever goes in; the Emery's consider the effects of radiant and pulsating T.V. light which closes down the conscious brain and knocks out the decision making functions which enable one to switch off. To "view consciously" and critically, one has to resist the basic electrical response of the brain to the T.V. medium. Moreover, advertisers and programmers use highly sophisticated techniques to keep us in front of the T.V.

Clearly, young children are highly vulnerable to both the medium of T.V. and its methods, and therefore need protection from it until "conscious viewing" is possible.

# Chapter Four

## *The Path of Child Development*

Before a new technology or drug is brought into widespread use, an attempt nowadays is made to assess objectively what its side effects, its consequences for people and for the environment will be. For example such an innovation as the microchip is being currently debated, with the intention of minimising its negative side effects and maximising its potential benefits. In the future there is some hope that full 'environmental impact statements' will be prepared about all such innovations. Whilst it is harder to do this for drugs already in widespread use, some, such as tobacco products, have now to carry a government health warning. Likewise an impact statement on the effects of television on children may need to be made.

However, before these effects can be described, the process of child development needs to be sketched. It is necessary to bear in mind this path of child development when discussing television, especially as much conventional educational practice is based on deciding what is the earliest age one can expect a child to attain the faculties normal in adults rather than asking how does the child differ in his consciousness and accomplishments at specific ages from the adult. It is differing attitudes which lead to different kinds of observations. Those who are used to assuming that children have the same relationship to their sensory apparatus as adults will make different kinds of observations from those seeking to understand how differently children experience sense impressions at the various stages of development on the path to adult maturity.

Teachers, parents, doctors, counsellors and social workers all have some kind of map of the developmental path children tread from birth, babyhood, infancy, childhood through to adolescence and young adulthood. The insight such maps provide gives a guide to which activities, experiences, situations, and events will be appropriate for a child at a particular stage of his development. Above all, the question most asked by teachers and parents is: 'What activities will help this child benefit fully from *this* stage of development, and enable him to take the next step?'

As some facets of child development will be referred to in more detail in later chapters when considering the developmental effects of television, an overview of the main stages in the child's life will be given.

## Phases of child development : babies and toddlers

The first human life phases may be looked at as a series of unfolding births which the growing child undergoes – births that are accompanied by a process of becoming increasingly independent – physically and psychologically – from the environment. Each 'birth' initiates the development of the new physical and psychological possibilities which characterise the emerging phases.

The most obvious birth is the physical birth from the mother, although the baby will take a few years to become emotionally independent from her. For the first few years of life, the baby, toddler and infant is tenderly open to the environment, as if he was like a sense organ which is influenced by every happening around him.

Dr Leboyer, in *Birth Without Violence* describes how sensitive the new-born baby is to noise, bright lights, rough movements and rough handling with cold or warm hands.[1] He maintains that through providing a gentle environment for the birth, similar to the dark, warm, gravity-free womb with its constant reassurance of the maternal heart beat, which is being left, the entry into the physical world is eased. Babies and young children, then, are all 'sense organs' – like punching a sack of flour, every impression is registered by them.

The newborn baby is open, sensitive and vulnerable – an 'unfinished animal' He is now dependent on the care of his parents and on the quality of his environment for his further development.

The only defence of babies against troublesome sense-impressions is to sleep or to cry, escape being impossible. Their task is to learn to filter and organise sense impressions – for example they take one or two months to smile or cry in response to parental attention. The baby's body becomes his toy to be explored, chewed, sucked and felt – along with other objects and people. With the ability to sit up, he can handle things and focus on objects at some distance. The observation of a baby quivering all over with the enjoyment of being nursed, or grasping a beloved object or seeing a parent can be an object-lesson in sensory enjoyment.

With crawling and standing up, the vertical dimension is explored — as also happens when baby drops things from his high chair for others to pick up. It is with enjoyment and concentration that he begins to walk.

During the first years the acquiring of motor skills — to hold up the head, to sit up unsupported, to manipulate the arms, hands and legs, to roll over, to crawl, to feed and to stand — results in the patterning of the growing brain and developing the responses of the central nervous system.[2]

These motor skills need to be exercised when the baby wishes. Parents who hold, cuddle, play with and stimulate their baby help its development. Babies that are left alone too much, or are overstimulated, or left near the television, may suffer as a consequence.

## The toddler

When the baby first walks and becomes a toddler, a necessary condition for his well-being is that of trust in the goodness and support of his parents. The toddler is an experimenter in movement — climbing, rolling, running (before walking), lurching drunkenly into things, practising jumps, leaning and toppling over.

The toddler learns through the power of imitation — he imitates the adults and children around him instinctively. To see my two year old son and six year old daughter imitating my wife and myself so exactly is hilarious entertainment, like watching oneself in a mirror; they catch the exact gestures, intonations, favourite family expressions and mannerisms, for young children soak up experiences like blotting paper — they absorb all the habits, feelings, tensions, joys, sorrows and behaviour of the adults they imitate. Children with violent parents will tend to copy violence, those with loving parents will tend to imitate that behaviour.

Toddlers are great explorers of their surroundings, their fingers and tongues are busy opening cupboards, tipping out the contents, feeling different textures, messing about with sand and water, experimenting with things. They need to experience at first hand the reality and 'goodness' of the world — to touch, taste, smell, hear, see and feel their environment.

The first three years of life see the growing child learning to walk, to speak and to think. It has been said that more is learnt by a child in his first three years than in all subsequent life!

The development of language and speech emerges from the primeval 'babble' of babies and the mutual language of love, closeness and signs between parents and child. A real person wanting to communicate with a baby is the pre-condition for language development. Young children can only learn to speak in contact with real people speaking.

From babble, signs, and gesture emerges the ability of a baby to imitate a specific sound, and then the utterance of some syllables at around a year old. The inner world of what the toddler hears and understands, which will become the basis of thinking, is continually enriched by the people around having real conversations with him and with each other.

In the second year, toddlers may start 'naming' things — like Adam walking around in the Garden of Eden — gaining great delight from this. Words are played with simply from the joy of sound and the delight of muscular activity of tongue that is required. Our own children enjoy deliberately using sound words like 'basgetti' for spaghetti.

When in about the third year, a child begins to say 'I' to himself — 'I want' instead of 'want' or 'Paul want' — he has named himself as the centre of his experiences, feelings and behaviour. The child's inner language and speech continue to develop so that words are increasingly used to communicate feelings, replacing the old sign language. The full development of speech and language may normally take up to the age of six or seven.

The first three years are crucial to a person throughout his life. Sensory, emotional and physical deprivation will retard children, whilst over-stimulation will make them nervy, discontented and restless. Whatever sense impressions the baby and toddler experience will be built right into their sensitive organisms, since unlike adults they cannot filter or screen out unwanted information.

Dr Eva Frommer, a Child Psychiatrist working at St. Thomas' Hospital, London writes that: —

> ...if ugliness, chaos, and mental squalor surround the child, he will in turn absorb and take these as his standards in life for what is acceptable. If he has cheap and hideous toys and only comic style books, or indeed no plaything or books, in the house, this can also become the accepted pattern for the whole of his future

life and that of his future family...What surrounds our littlest children gives them the pattern for what will be acceptable as their world.

The physical and human environment in which parents choose to bring up their children has far-reaching effects. If parents choose to put their baby to sleep in front of the television, as is often done – or choose to leave their two year old to the mercy of fast-paced electronic imagery on television when they are still 'all sense-organ' this will have deep-rooted effects.

## The infant : 3—6 years — a time to play

Since each phase of childhood needs to unfold in an all round way in order that the foundation for the next phase can be fully prepared, this account is a general map rather than one which will fit individuals. Each child develops at his or her own pace – although the time when walking, speaking, thinking and the ability to say 'I' is usually accomplished is around the third birthday.

The infant gradually acquires his physical independence, mobility and co-ordination in the world. He can dress himself, tie shoelaces, wash, sleep all night without being wet – by the age of five or six. All kinds of play activities are engaged in – for an infant's work is his play. What adults are doing – such as cleaning the house, washing up, gardening, digging, driving, cooking, child care and baking – is imitated and the subject of his play. Instinctive imitation gives way to the magic of playing. A sheepskin rug is transformed into a boat, a green sheet becomes its sail, the chair a mast and the carpet the sea. A piece of plasticine turns into a hearing aid for dolly, a straw becomes a stethoscope to play doctors with. Bits and pieces, old clothes, old dolls are juggled with in all kinds of imaginative ways. Real-life dolls or exact copies of objects tend to stultify the imaginative magic that can be wrought by infants on a few pieces of cloth. This playing is hard work – as any adult who has tried to play along with them for a time will acknowledge.

Infancy needs songs, rhymes and stories that lead children practically and imaginatively into a deeper relationship with the earth, stones, plants, trees, animals and people around them. The time-honoured nursery rhymes, games, songs and stories seem to have been custom-built for infants to acquire a wide vocabulary, a sense of rhythm, a sense for numbers, a feel for language and a deepened imagination.

Conversations with adults become important. It is necessary for them to answer children's incessant questions carefully but not with pedantic information. The incessant 'why' stage and the repetitive question, which can be so irritating to a busy or preoccupied adult, is not so much the asking for information, but the need for reassurance which repetition gives. Then come the 'why, where, when, how, and what' questions stemming from a bubbling interest in people and in life. In a busy day there may not be much time for such brief conversations — although mealtimes often afford a good opportunity. I find with my son and daughter that they need to talk before going to sleep, to look over the day and to discuss troublesome or special things.

Physically the infant becomes more independent of his parents, and begins to meet the world directly, on its own terms. Movement in space is conquered as motor skills are refined, manual dexerity emerges with such activities as painting or block building, balance is acquired and the left-right orientation is gradually learnt.

Socially, new habits are acquired as the infant becomes more self-aware — conscious of himself and his place amongst his friends in the playgroup or in the home. He has to get on with others, to play together with other children, to become used to a little brother or sister, to relate to mother and father in new ways.

A sense of time has to be cultivated. From birth onwards, the baby has to learn to sleep and wake. This is the first activity of rhythmic time sequencing. Personal adult memory generally only goes back to the period when as a child one can first say 'I' to oneself.

There are, of course, exceptions, a notable one being H.M. Stanley who could recall floating in the room right up to the face of the blue and white china clock high up on the kitchen wall and looking back at himself in the cradle. Only in later years of life are early memories available to be called up at will. Each day is a complete unity in itself for the child, and his sense of identity is fostered when the same sequence of events takes place regularly, as time for children is as vast as space. Most of us can recall how long it was from one birthday to the next, from Christmas to Christmas. It is the rhythm of regular habits, the progression of one season to the next which gradually establishes the dawning sense of self within the changing pattern of life.

## The child : 6—12 years

Having mastered his physical body and played his way into the world, the infant undergoes a 'life crisis' in the sixth or seventh year. This is marked by the loss of the milk teeth and the second dentition. During the child's first seven years his energies have been largely involved in forming, organising, and mastering his physical body. By six or seven the physical organisation and neuromuscular functions are complete, which releases the architectural, biological forces for other purposes. These liberated forces are taken up into the child's life of picture-thinking and of imagination. At this stage the child can begin to separate an object which he sees from the inner picture or idea he has of it. He can separate his imagination from the things he is playing with, for example, he can begin to represent more characteristically in his drawing the house or person he has in mind. This liberation of forces hitherto devoted to physical growth and development can be described as another birth — the birth of a more independent imagination and a capacity to place thoughts in a sequence which is more understandable to the logically thinking adult. Interestingly enough, this comes just after the brain's maximum rate of growth for the early years has been reached, for this begins to slow down from five or six years of age.

Traditionally the time for school proper, for learning to read, to write and work with numbers was in the seventh year. Piaget's observations and Steiner's ideas about this time of 'school readiness' of children support this tradition.(4) Just as children need space and time to learn to walk, to speak and to play before extra demands are made on them, so children's intellectual development should not be forced prematurely before their growth forces which are becoming available for thinking and imagination are fully free from their organic work in the body. Learning to read and to write too early, therefore, may leave subtle weaknesses in the growing bodies of children.

Development then unfolds through the 'heart of childhood' phase, from seven to eleven years approximately. Heightened creative possibilities abound in this period, as children's imaginative capacities come to the fore. Children grow out of the learning through imitation and play phase, towards creating together artistically in manifold ways. The imaginative life is exceedingly vivid, there being a thirst for stories, thus fairy tales, fables, myths and legends are a source of rich material for children's developing inner life. At this stage, children are extremely susceptible to pictures, hence the magnetic attraction of picture books, comics and above all, television – something of which commercial interests particularly take full advantage.

Children's creative capacities should be encouraged in all kinds of ways, through playacting, story telling, painting, music, crafts, modelling and games for example.

It is partly through games that children learn about social life, about how to make, break and change the rules of different games, to prepare for the great 'game' of social life.

Language develops beyond a toy, as Piaget describes its use in early years, and as a medium for giving commands in the process of playing, into a social means of communication about feelings, likes and dislikes. A feeling for poetry, rhyme and meaning, often entrenched in the age-old jingles of 'children's culture', emerges.

The birth of likes and dislikes – of the emotional world – encourages children to explore such opposites as good-bad, beautiful-ugly, rich and poor in their feelings. Through stories, plays or games, children learn to clarify their own shades of feeling and personal values within the inner realm of feeling which is opening up. Just as once the world of space and time was explored in infancy so now the world of feeling is being charted.

A consequence of this imaginative exploration of feeling is a dawning sense of morality, of what is right. Infants cannot understand why an action is wrong, although a four year old will agree to what a loved grownup says is right or wrong. For such a child, breaking three plates accidentally may be 'more wrong' than breaking one deliberately. Later, at 6 or 7, children may still accept adult judgements about right or wrong actions – but will be helped, for example, by imaginative stories about how the friend felt from whom they stole a beloved toy. Instead of dogmatic moral statements, children need to experience in their feelings the hurt, loss or tears caused in others by their actions. This prepares the way for being able to feel personally responsible for actions, to be able to reason about right and wrong, and the acquiring of standards of behaviour after the ninth year.

The ninth year crisis shows itself in such phenomena as children wondering if parents are really theirs, in trying out teacher's authority, in doubt and in feelings of aloneness. The world of imagination and of outer reality split apart – there is no magic formula for transforming the world imaginatively any more. The child experiences himself on an island – as a more independent self – an experience prefacing the development of a mature adult individuality much later on. Children need help in achieving a more conscious relationship between the factual world, and their inner world — through a loving but realistic study of animals or plants for example. Trust and confidence need to be re—established with teachers and parents on a new level, one that recognises that these adults are perhaps not omniscient after all.

Successfully encountered, the ninth year crisis brings to a child a greater awareness of past, present and future — of the consequences of actions. The moral sense of conscience begins to develop. Time takes on a new dimension, he can relate happenings from the past and connect them with the future...'When I was little,' comes into the conversational vocabulary, 'When I'm twelve' — a milestone of huge dimensions of freedom — 'I'll be able to do...'

Moral perception, the sense of conscience, begins to appear and this needs to be fostered by stories, by biographies and history, for example, the problems Moses had in guiding the Children of Israel to the promised land; the troubles of the Norse Gods with Loki, never knowing whether he was helping or hindering their purposes. The time-honoured account of Alfred and the cakes highlights dramatically the problems of justice and objectivity in social encounters. Out of imaginative pictures the social sensitivity of the growing child can be prepared so that adjustment can be made to the critical faculties of the growing intellect that heralds approaching puberty.

Eva Frommer summarises the years from seven to ten as follows:

> So during these four years, the child traverses immense fields of experience which are open to him only at this time, and at no other, in quite such a natural way. They teach him about feelings and ill feelings; they teach him about the living world as part of himself, of his own experience; they teach him about his fellows. And in him there grows the need to become a fellow-man and live, learn and work together as well as commune with his kind. Lastly, at the end of this period, he comes rather abruptly to a meeting with himself, standing between his inner and his outer life, and seeking a bridge. This is indeed an epic journey and requires the right understanding, guidance and companionship from the adults who are responsible for his care.[5]

At eleven and twelve, children are on the threshold of a new phase of experience — that of puberty and of adolescence. Unless puberty has been already encountered, there is a unique grace and poise which characterises children of this age. The great creative talents and verve of the 'heart of childhood' period continue to thrive, while the ability to think more logically and objectively may be developing strongly. Traditionally, the twelfth year was the time children made a transition to the more intellectually oriented secondary school, a change which coincided with the emergence of the logical faculties. Physiologically, this is paralleled by the structural and biochemical maturation of the brain at around twelve, when for example, the left and right hemispheres are usually specialized.

## Conclusion

Since the main focus of this book is on the effects of television on children, space prevents even a summary of teenage development. Since many teenagers begin to watch television less than children, the problem may not be so pronounced. Also, if a child has watched relatively little or no television, the teenage years may offer opportunities for acquiring greater discrimination about programme choice, for understanding the medium through media studies and through making video programmes at school.

However, since by the age of twelve or so the senses and brain have matured to a certain level — although this maturing continues more slowly through the teenage years — our account of child development will be concluded. Certain aspects of these twelve crucial years will be high-lighted in dealing with the effects of television. Anyone, however, who is interested in exploring child development more fully might be interested in reading Dr. Eva Frommer's *Voyage Through Childhood Into the Adult World*, or Rahima Baldwin's, *You are Your Child's First Teacher*[6]

Given the path of child development outlined in this chapter — a path about which more and more is being discovered — what effects does television watching have on children? Does television help or hinder children's development? What are the consequences of television for the early years of childhood?

# Chapter Five

## *Blunted senses*

*'Television is sensory deprivation': Jerry Mander*

Recently, I watched an eleven year old boy spend a long time observing the movements of a field mouse in a hedge. He followed every movement intently, and was thrilled at what he saw. On another occasion, I was with a ten year old boy, showing him one of Britain's wildest, most beautiful rivers which threads its way through the forests of the Welsh borders. Seeing a Peregrine falcon circling the vantage rock we were on, I asked a birdwatcher where the nest was. He invited me to look through his powerful telescope at a pair of Peregrines who were nesting in a nearby cliff. The boy looked briefly through the telescope with little interest, hardly *saw* anything and was certainly not touched by the experience. He was a heavy viewer, with his own set, with access to videos and a home computer for games. The contrast between the observational skills of the two children was stark.

The aim of this chapter is to examine the effects of the T.V. medium on the child's developing senses and nervous systems.

William Wordsworth wrote of his experience when as a boy:—

> There was a time when meadow, grove and stream,
> The earth and every common sight,
> To me did seem
> Apparelled in celestial light,
> The glory and the freshness of a dream

On growing older, the poet observes, 'The things which I have seen I now can see no more'. The youth who perceives the 'vision splendid' of nature, at length, as a man sees 'it die away — And fade into the light of common day'.

When we consider the openness of children to all that happens, to their powers of absorption and selfless imitation, we can appreciate the vital part their senses play in this. Just as food nourishes the physical organism, so the experiences of touch, warmth, movement, sight, sound, taste, smell and well-being bring the world to the attention of the child. The exercise of the senses also nourishes the central nervous system and the brain, which enables the developing child to wake up into the world around her.

When children are brought up in an environment where their senses cannot develop in a healthy way, they do not thrive, as for example in formal institutions. Children who are cuddled, played with, conversed with and who experience a stimulating home life are more likely to thrive.

Our sensory experiences support our ideas, feeling and actions – even our sense of identity. This was shown dramatically in experiments with volunteers undergoing 'sensory deprivation' conditions, as a preparation for manned space flights in the United States. People floated motionless in water at blood heat, in total silence, wearing goggles that totally excluded light, and gloves which reduced the sense of touch. Initially, many volunteers fell asleep. On waking, some experienced hallucinations, fantasies, dreams, and distorted impressions of their bodies, as for example their arms or legs growing and floating away. Such experiments demonstrated how vital normal sensory experience is to maintain a balanced state of mind.

Given the importance of healthy sense experience for our normal functioning, and the far more vivid nature of children's sense experience, what effects does television watching have on sensory development?

When watching television, a young child may be in a darkened room – the light of day is screened out. He is motionless, which is an uncharacteristic state for a child, whose natural condition is one of continual play activity and movement. (An athlete reputed to have imitated all the actions of a three year old was exhausted in a short time – the child, however, was still as fresh as a daisy.) Whilst watching television the child is sitting down, the eyes are fixed, hardly move and are slightly defocussed.

The senses in use to watch television are sight and hearing. The other senses are largely unnecessary, so while children are watching television they are making little all–round use of their senses. The effects of this lack of use will be explored later. At this stage, however, the obvious point to make is that children who are playing and active will have more opportunities to develop their senses than children spending the same time watching television. The television children may find it harder to 'come to their senses' since they are subjected to a medium which largely deprives them of a rich sensory diet. A common reaction of someone discovering that my own children rarely watch television is 'What do you *do* instead? What do you *watch*? Aren't you depriving them of so many experiences?'

Indeed, we are 'depriving' our children of many television experiences — because these are 'second-hand' experiences. I believe that for children an ounce of real experience is worth a ton of secondhand experience. This point was well made in a cartoon showing a child watching a sunset on television, whilst exactly the same sunset could be seen through the window.

To nourish the development of young children's senses is relatively simple. They need to touch and feel everything around them. Infants go through a stage of 'playing with their food'. By imitating the activities of adults, such as sweeping, baking, gardening and tidying, infants discover the everyday world.

As an infant's work is his play all the varied activities in home and garden, at the seaside, of building things, of playing games such as 'mummies and daddies', 'hospitals' or 'trains' — all call on the senses.

Children deprived of rich sensory experiences need to have play therapy in the nursery school. Teachers may have to put such children through a crash 'course' of such activities as water play, sand play, feeling things and mixing dough. This new phenomenon of the 'play-deprived child' has been observed by many nursery teachers. According to teachers, play-deprivation is not primarily connected with a child's socio-economic background, but rather with the amount of television-watching in the family.

Whilst many people may concede that excessive television-watching can deprive children of more healthy sense experiences, they may not readily agree that television *is* sensory deprivation. However, this was demonstrated dramatically by the Emerys, who compared brainwave patterns of television viewers to those undergoing a lengthy sensory deprivation period of ninety-six hours. The brainwave patterns on the electro-encephalograph showed that a person watching television for a few minutes was as seriously affected as someone subjected to a period of ninety six hours sensory deprivation.[1]

Before examining the effects of television on the senses more closely, let us look at the positive aspects of their care and development.

## *The care and development of the senses*[2]

Traditionally, there were five senses attributed to the human being, plus a 'sixth' sense added by hearsay. Physiologists have included a few more, such as the senses of balance and of movement, whilst several 'social senses' such as the 'sense of identity', or a 'sense of language and meaning' have been suggested. Each sense provides us with a window on the world, and we experience reality through a 'circle' of such windows as we pay more attention to one sense and then another.

The more bodily senses give us an immediate experience of our organism. Balance enables us to experience our bodies in space; touch sketches the boundary of our skin; the sense of life tells us how we are feeling – whether we are well or out of sorts, and the sense of movement brings the perception of the motions of the body's muscles, limbs or joints. Balance, touch, movement and well-being involve us deeply in our own bodily experiences – we trust what these senses tell us.

The senses of taste and smell enable us to find out about substances outside our bodies – in very personal ways since each person develops his own 'sense of taste'. With sight we perceive colours, light and shade in our surroundings. For many people, 'seeing is believing', although more doubting people, like St. Thomas, may rely on their sense of touch for conclusive information. Another sense, the sense of warmth, tells us about relationships between warmer and colder things in the environment – about whether we ourselves are gaining or losing warmth from the surroundings.

Whilst sight and warmth take us into the environment, the sense of hearing enables us to penetrate into the heart of things. The tone of a bell informs us about the quality of such materials from which it is made. The eyes may be deceived in trying to discover the material of which an object is made, but if it produces a sound, any deception is uncovered and we recognise if it is made of plastic, metal or wood.

Since the sense of hearing enables us to communicate with other people, it is above all a social sense. It is complemented by other 'social senses' which, whilst difficult to pin down physiologically, yet are essential if a person is to participate in social life. There is the sense of word, which enables us to perceive the gestures, movements and patterns which are shaped by a speaker into a stream of sounds. This sense gives us a 'feeling for language', and even if we do not understand what is being said we recognise that it 'makes sense' and is not gibberish. Lastly, there is a subtle sense of 'feel' for the other as a person, as an identity, which can be experienced when 'making contact' with someone. These latter three senses of hearing, of word and of the sense of the 'I' of another person are very dependent on social life for their development and conversely without these there is no social life to develop them.[3]

In the course of growing up through nursery, primary and secondary education the different senses need to be nurtured more strongly according to the children's stages of development. Many activities in playgroups, nursery and infant schools are usually practical — such as household tasks, cooking, constructing things, simple arts and crafts. Materials, substances, playthings and an environment of a sound kind have a positive influence, since it is through the senses that the world around is taken up into the child's experience — hence the importance of first-hand experiences with honest materials. Such an early environment creates security of trust in the world, for life. If children experience materials or objects which are a kind of lie — removed from real first-hand experience — then this produces an insecurity in the child, especially in trusting what the senses bring to him.

In the primary and middle schools, children need to be exercised artistically if their senses are to be fully developed. Through painting, which is of crucial importance to children, the world of colour, movement and warmth becomes a central experience for them. Music, language, art and poetry exercise the finer senses, whilst modelling or crafts enliven particularly the 'will' senses of movement, touch and balance. For it is artistic activities which awaken and develop the senses in a healthy way. Children need to experience the beauty of the world.

At secondary level, when teenagers become much more able to perceive in a detached way, science may help the capacity for accurate, objective observation to develop. The arts — especially if used in a social way as in modern drama teaching — may be of real help in exploring relationships and in awakening the social senses. Above all, teenagers need the experience that 'the world is true'.

## Television's effects on the senses

Young children, in the process of discovering the world, are faced with the problem of 'sensing' if television pictures are 'real' or not, if there is in fact a man in the box or if the screen is a window on a different world. Reports of certain primitive people's responses to cinema films – of being very concerned about where the actor has gone once he leaves the screen – demonstrate the initial confusion technology has on unsophisticated adults. From this we can envisage how puzzling television must be to children who are just becoming aware of the differences and variety of sensory experience. My three year old son asks, 'Is there really an orchestra in the box?' or 'Is that man really dead?'

Television is a deceptive medium to place in reach of children as they are learning find their way in the everyday world and are developing a general 'sense' of its reality. Think of the contrast between live puppets and a show produced on the T.V. screen. The live performance holds children spellbound, they can see the puppets and can enter the 'make believe' world of the story in a complete and uncontradictory way. But television puts over a vast number of images, people, and happenings that are artificial, second-hand reproductions of things taking place at a distance. Furthermore many events happening on the screen – the technical tricks, the cartoon antics, all the artificial unusualness used to attract the viewer – cannot take place in real life.

So young children are faced with a 'real world' which they need to get used to through the normal development of the senses, and a television world where events happen which are unknown and often impossible in everyday life.

A mother described an incident with her five year old stepdaughter who is a tele-addict:

> About six months ago she ran into the road and was hit by a car, and fortunately escaped with one bruise and shock. A few hours after the accident she asked me what had happened and I explained, telling her that she was a very lucky girl. I asked 'what would have happened if you had fallen under the wheels?' and she answered. 'I'd jump up again like the Pink Panther!'

Such incidents prompt one to ask whether television is severely handicapping the development of a sense of reality – the generalised outcome of the exercise of all the senses in exploring the world – in young children. One father, on taking his young son to the zoo to see the animals was so disturbed by such comments as 'I've already seen all this on television!' – that he got rid of television altogether. Reality, he concluded, cannot compete with a box which shows close-ups of tigers, lions and rhinos, scenes which one never meets in ordinary life in such rapid succession. He also felt that television was dulling his child's sense of wonder.

It may be argued that young children watching a minimum of television, say twenty minutes a day, will develop a good feel for what is 'real' and what is not. However, just as children brought up bilingually from the start (with no initial 'mother tongue' as a basis) may later show signs of insecurity, or children with no developed preference for right or left handed orientations may show uncertainty — so children subjected to the 'television world' of second-hand reality alongside the ordinary world, may develop a lack of trust in their senses, and therewith a subtle doubt in the world. For maladjusted, handicapped and disturbed children this doubt may be magnified when responding to life situations.

## Television and sight

The most important sense which television affects is our sense of sight. Its organ, the eye, responds to colour, light and darkness on the one hand and movement on the other. In fact, movement and balance — two other distinct senses — are intimately connected with the eye. One's eye is in continual movement busy gauging distance, height and depth which are the essential elements of perspective. The eyes are perpetually fixing objects in their vision, accommodating and shifting their focus. It takes time to learn how to perceive objects, for example a two year old will recognise again a triangle that has been rotated 120 degrees, only after rotating his head also — visual exploration is therefore a prerequisite of seeing. In adults, perception is dependent on all kinds of exploratory eye movements, from consciously directed ones to involuntary small ones which shift the image over the fovea when the eye seems fixated on a motionless object. Interestingly, in the context of television's effects on the eye, when such scanning motions are artifically suppressed, the image breaks up into fragments. We need to 'finger over the visual field with our gaze' as one physiologist observed.

Constant eye movement is required for a healthy eye. Lack of eye movement may be a symptom of ageing, and eye specialists can give exercises to help older people keep their eyes 'young'.[4]

For focusing we need conscious attention, vigilance and concentration, in short, we have to exert ourselves to co-operate with the faculties this sense provides for us.

Attention is needed for good observation and focalisation. William James wrote that, 'everyone knows what attention is...Focalisation, concentration of consciousness are of its essence. It is a condition which has a real opposite in the confused, dazed, 'scatterbrained state which in French is called distraction.' Such attention requires effort and cannot be 'sustained for more than a few seconds at a time'.[5]

Television watching is one of the most visually passive activities. One's head is stationary, the eyes are practically motionless and do not continually move to get 'fixes' on objects as for normal sight, and they are slightly 'defocused' to take in the whole screen. The accent is on peripheral vision rather than on central vision which is active in the state of attention described above. Another effect is that, whilst watching television one's eye muscles are not being exercised and one's vigilance is decreased through the necessary defocusing of the eyes. There is little need for accommodating eye movement − or rather, this is kept at a constant level to make up for the nature of television which is a slightly blurred, low definition medium (compared with the clearer image of cinema films, for example).[6] Some ophthalmologists recommend T.V. viewing for post-operative eye patients, just to keep the eyes stilled.

Apart from affecting the eye's mechanics in such a drastic fashion, television affects people's attention. The Emerys maintain that television both 'destroys the capacity of the viewer to attend', and also 'by taking over a complex of direct and indirect neural pathways, decreases vigilance'. They say that the television watching state of mind is a form of distraction, as opposed to concentration and focalisation.

Furthermore, the Emerys write that in spite of the high volume of content and information coming from the television, the mechanics of eye and brain receive this input as if it were a simple visual stimulus. Television is therefore an impoverished sensory environment.[7]

The foregoing arguments may lead to the conclusion that television affects children's vigilance, attention and concentration adversely. In addition, it may have harmful effects on children's eyesight if viewed at close range for over an hour a day.

So far we have been discussing effects applying specifically to the mature senses of adults. But how does television affect babies' and toddlers' developing sense of sight?

The perceptual world is not a finished product which is the same for everyone, but it is shaped according to a person's age. Children's experiences happen in a vivid world in which things are attractive and repulsive before they focus into abstract qualities like squareness or blackness. Piaget showed how optical illusions decrease with age, and how children's perception of space develops. For the first few months objects do not 'exist' if they are not moving or doing something. Holding or manipulating an object gives it reality, and when it disappears, it is gone for good. Space, like 'mouth space' or 'grasping space' is separate and related to activity.

At the eighth to tenth month, the object is seen to be more independent. Piaget offered a watch to a nine month old, who played with it. When it was hidden under a pillow, the baby fetched it. Even though the baby saw the watch being hidden in a different place the second time he still looked in the first hiding place.

At about sixteen months, the toddler perceives the object as having permanence independent of himself. Space becomes a field in which things happen, as opposed to being bound up with activity. Perhaps the game of 'peek-a-boo' is a way for babies and toddlers to get used to seeing loved ones come and go, yet still feeling they are 'there'.[8]

The sense of sight continues to develop, and it is only at around the age of twelve that the sense for perspective emerges. From the standpoint of perceptual development, therefore, television may seriously harm the acquiring of such concepts as space by infants. Furthermore, the two-dimensional screen inhibits the development of a sense of depth and perspective.

## Listening and observing

Some nursery teachers I know tell me that they have to teach children to listen. The teachers who taught in pre-television days remember how at the mention of a story, children would immediately respond and *listen*.

Nowadays, although most children still love stories, their attention-span is shorter and a minority find it hard to listen at all. But as soon as such children begin to 'make their own inner pictures' of the story, they are able to listen; however, teacher friends comment on how much *better* story-tellers they need to be nowadays to hold children's attention.

Presumably, the background sound of radio, cassette or television at home is so prevalent that the sense of hearing is dulled. Since television is more visual than aural, and unless adults converse with children and tell them stories, children's sense of hearing is not being fully exercised.

Observational skills may also not be developed by viewing — hence the need to help children *see* flowers, animals, and birds. Many infant, kindergarten and junior teachers I know have observed a "withdrawal" from the senses in moderate and heavy viewing children. They therefore need to teach therapeutically to cultivate the ability to 'see a world in a grain of sand'. Some have been worried by the dulling of the colour sense, and point to the over-stimulating "loud" colour television medium.

## Viewing and movement

Some older teachers can still distinguish the "viewers" from "non-viewers" in a class, by their posture, limb control and how they sit. Audrey McAllen, a special education advisor, wrote on movement and television: —

> After many years of working with children who have learning difficulties one sees clearly how unconnected the present day child is with the interaction of hands and limbs. They do not bother to lift their legs high enough to throw a ball under them, the hand collides with the thigh. Also the left leg seems heavier than the right and harder for them to lift. When classes have been screened for learning problems, this symptom of limb heaviness is now general among children. Over the last years it has become apparent that the children born in the 1960's take longer to respond to therapy than those born earlier.[9]

Since the other senses are hardly required by television, there remains its effect on the nervous system.

## Television closes down the human nervous system

The Emerys propose that 'television as a simple, constant, repetitive and ambiguous visual stimulus gradually closes down the nervous system of man'. If this is what happens to adults when viewing, how much more serious must the effects of television be on the developing brains of children?

Is it healthy to expose children, with sensitive, impressionable senses and nervous systems to such a powerful medium as television?

Researchers into the development and functioning of the left and right hemisphere of the brain are only beginning to consider the effects of T.V. One good reason to minimise viewing at an early age is to safeguard children until they are developed enough neurologically as teenagers, to handle the T.V. medium.

To recap, in chapter three it was mentioned that in an adult's brains the left and right hemispheres have distinct, specialized functions. Each hemisphere governs the activities of the opposite side of the body. The right hemisphere, for instance, controls the movements of your left hand.

The "critical" left brain can process one stimulus at a time. This leads to orderly thought sequences, linear thinking, analysis, distinguishing parts. The verbal and logical functions are important. The right brain can process whole clusters of stimuli at once, leading to a grasp of complex wholes — such as a face. The processes of thinking in images and pictures are important. As mentioned previously, viewing tunes out the left brain.

According to the Emerys, in adults subjected to electro-encephalographs whilst watching television, the left hemisphere is hardly active at all, registering a minimal holding pattern. They suggest that, 'viewing is at the conscious level of somnambulism'. The right hemisphere does register the television images, although since the cross-referencing of our subconscious intelligence between left and right has been "knocked out", these cannot easily be brought to consciousness. Hence the difficulty most people have in recalling much information from a programme.

Other researchers into brainwave patterns whilst watching television confirm the Emerys' findings. Dr Eric Peper is a Professor of Interdisciplinary Sciences at San Francisco State University. He claims that the alpha wave patterns which rapidly become dominant whilst watching are a sign of being 'in a totally passive condition and (being) unaware of the world outside of the pictures which one is seeing. The right phrase for alpha wave patterns is really 'spaced-out'. Not orienting. "When someone pays attention to something external, such alpha wave patterns disappear"[10]

Whilst adults may choose to administer the plug-in-drug to themselves to become 'spaced-out', what effects does it have on the developing brains of children?

Babies have unspecialized brains, indeed it is only at about twelve that the left and right sides are fully specialized as in adults. Babies seem to have some sort of 'non-verbal thought', for example they recognise human faces.

In the second year, toddlers learn to speak and language comes to the fore. At this time each brain hemisphere is apparently equally mature verbally-lesions in the left side are no more harmful to language development than on the right side, and vice versa. Similar lesions in the left hemispheres of adults might cause significant linguistic problems.

As language develops, presumably the brain specializes into the two hemispheres of verbal and or non-verbal thinking. Learning increasingly comes from verbal activities.

However, television in the early years when the brain is so malleable and sensitive, prolongs the dominance of the non-verbal 'right hemisphere' functions. The trance-like state of many child viewers, especially if induced for 20—30 hours per week, may seriously inhibit the development of the verbal-logical 'left hemisphere' activities.

Furthermore, children exposed to television — a medium which prolongs the dominance of non-verbal 'right' hemisphere activities — may not take full advantage of the pecular 'language sensitive' period of infancy. Just as there are 'tides in the affairs of men' so there are tides of 'readiness' in the child's development, for example, language readiness. If a child does not learn to speak during this period of readiness, it may be hard for him to make up for this deficiency later on.

Local, Gloucestershire health visitors and speech therapists are concerned about the increasing numbers of young children who can hardly speak. What appear to be speech impairments, are in fact children who have had little family conversation, no nursery rhymes, and whose parents prefer dummies (pacifiers) and television.

Babies, toddlers and infants may have their feeling for commitment to language eroded by television. Since the best conditions for learning language are conversing with real people, and since television is a linguistically inadequate, if not a retarding medium in this respect, as no child can converse with it, then young children could well do without it. At a stage in their development when children soak up new experiences like sponges, television prolongs their dependence on the non-verbal 'right hemisphere', hinders the appetite for language and produces 'spaced out' states of mind.

When neurologists such as Dr. Eric Peper assert that 'television trains people only for being zombies' – it may be time to ask 'Do we want this state of consciousness to be induced in our children?'[10]

To conclude, viewing at an early age may hinder the development of the senses, such as sight, sound, movement – and, indeed, offers up a poor, second hand sensory diet. Over-stimulated, children may "withdraw from their senses", and need therapeutic exercises. The patterning the brain needs for language development is hindered by viewing.

# Chapter Six

## *Television light and health*

Questions are beginning to be asked in scientific circles about the effects of light, such as television light, on our health. Since there are as yet few hard facts on this subject, the information presented in this chapter may be regarded as somewhat speculative. Such scientists as Dr.John Ott, who has pioneered the field of health and light, are still regarded in ophthalmologists'circles as original but also perhaps eccentric. However, because many babies and infants are subjected to such a high 'television light diet', I believe it informative to include this chapter on the possible effects of television light on children's health.

Children are highly sensitive to the environment, and young children particularly are like sense organs who touch, taste and feel the world through and through. A toddler will quiver with delight at seeing a beloved object, a baby will taste the warmth and goodness of milk 'all over his body', or respond to a sound with his whole organism. Unlike adults, who can judge and think about the world on the basis of sense impressions and who screen out undesired sense stimuli — young children register every external change They are 'all sense organs'.

One of the first experiences babies have is of light, of seeing light and of being 'touched by light all over their bodies'. They are born 'into the light of day' from the maternal darkness of the womb.

Just as food nourishes the metabolism, and air nourishes the lungs with oxygen, light gives nourishment to human beings. Some people, we are told, eat little food but live 'on light and air'. Babies need light, especially daylight, a 'food', in order to thrive.

The nourishing effects of light were discovered recently when babies with jaundice were observed to recover more quickly near to windows, than in less well-illuminated parts of dormitories. Light is now given as a successful therapy for neo—natal jaundice. Light, whether daylight, blue light or full spectrum white light of a reasonable level — effectively reduces the bilirubin levels which are out of balance in such cases.

Rickets in infants is partly caused by a lack of vitamin D which is produced in the skin of the body with the help of daylight. This used to be more of a problem in industrial areas where a large percentage of daylight was screened out by air pollution. The cure is to take infants outside, to expose them to light.

Since light has such far-reaching effects on the organism, especially on the sensitive young child, care needs to be taken of the 'light environment' of babies. Leboyer, for example, recommends that lights be dimmed during childbirth, and that the newly-born be protected from bright lights. Over the first few weeks of life, babies should sleep in darkened rooms and be introduced slowly to daylight, and artificial light. This gives the delicate, sensitive eyes of babies the chance to become accustomed to light.

Dr. Leboyer underlines the 'sharpness and freshness' of the un-organised senses of newly-born babies, and how overwhelming their perceptions of the world are. These infantile perceptions make adults' senses look pale in comparison. He writes: –

> The baby has the same love, the same thirst for light that plants and flowers have. The baby is passionate about light, drunk with it. So much so, that we should offer it more slowly, with endless precautions. In fact, babies are so sensitive to light that they perceive it while still in the mother's womb. If a mother more than six months' pregnant is naked in sunlight, the baby within her sees it as a golden haze. And now this small creature, so sensitive to light, is suddenly thrust out of its dark lair, and eyes are exposed to floodlights. It screams, and not surprisingly … If our aim were to drive it mad with pain, we couldn't go about it better. The poor baby squeezes its eyes shut. But what help is the fragile, transparent barrier of its eyelids? The truth is that the new born baby is not blind, but blinded'.[1]

## Health and light

Eurfron Gwynne Jones, a television critic writing in the 'Guardian ', took me to task about what I wrote concerning the affects of artificial light in the original leaflet 'Television and Child Development'. She found the proposition that 'artificial light may affect children's health and vitality adversely', "plain ridiculous". That a well known scientist, Ott, had found that beans' growth in front of a television set was distorted into a vine-like form, with roots growing upwards out of the soil, meant little to her, no doubt because in a short pamphlet this might well be taken out of context.[2]

However, Ott is questioning whether the excessive absorption of artificial light − such as neon, and incandescent light − might well affect people physically. In fact it was Ott's work which had an influence on the substantial reduction in the amount of X-rays emitted from television sets, to under 0.5 milliroentgens per hour.[3]

Since one looks at light when watching television, Ott's question is a legitimate one to ask. Until a hundred years or so ago most of mankind used daylight as the major light source. This has been transformed by artificial lighting, and the effects have been hardly researched.

Television light is projected into our eyes by cathode ray guns behind the screen, powered by 25,000 kilovolts in colour sets, and 18,000 kilovolts in black and white sets. These guns shoot streams of electrons at the phospor dots on the screen. These beam light into the viewer's eyes. This directed light is projected *into* the viewer, rather than the viewer looking *at* the lighted screen.

Such light − and any light − has concrete physical effects on one's organism. According to Ott, the retina registers the light stimuli and on the one hand translates these into images which are carried to the brain, whilst on the other hand the light rays permeate (by the means of neurochemical pathways) the pineal ahd pituitary glands and then into the endocrine systems. The light thus 'nourishes' the organism biochemically. An analogy here is the plant which fixes energy directly out of light by means of photosynthesis. It is only gradually that babies become used to daylight and night time, to the cycle of day and night to which their waking and sleeping rhythm becomes adjusted.

Because many children watch television from twenty to thirty hours per week, and babies are commonly put in front of or near operating television sets, it is vital to discuss the possible effects of artificial light on their health.

It is interesting to note in passing that researchers have found that light affects the hormones, sexuality, fertility, growth and cell structures in experiments on animals.[4]

What, however, are the effects of artificial light on children, and are these harmful? First, let us explore the nature of light more.

## Daylight and artificial light

Daylight, particularly sunlight, is composed of a unique combination of light wavelengths. This unique composition of spectra, or radiant wave lengths of energy, is different from the various forms of artificial light, each of which only contain a narrow selection of spectra. Daylight and the forms of artificial light are different.

The change from humanity ingesting a diet of natural light, to a diet of predominantly artificial light has resulted in what Ott calls 'mal-illumination'. We get 'overdoses' of incandescent, fluorescent and television light, whereas we are 'starved' of natural light.

'Malillumination' may result in complaints such as lowered vitality, less resistance to disease and hyperactivity. It may contribute to aggressive behaviour, heart illness and cancer.[5]

Ott became famous through his work on X-rays and television. For example, the roots of beans grew upwards out of the earth when grown before a colour television set. Other roots became distorted and vine–like. Mice suffered cancerous lesions. Ott argues that even the low level of X-rays now permitted to emanate from television sets may be harmful.

Ott became interested in the effects of television radiation and light through reading an article called *Those Tired Children* in the November 6 1964 issue of *Time*. Two airforce doctors had found that the common symptoms of headaches, nerves, bad sleep patterns, vomiting and general fatigue amongst a group of thirty children might be related to their watching television from three to six hours on week days, and six to ten hours at weekends.

The doctors suggested the children stop watching, and in twelve cases where this was done, the symptoms disappeared within three weeks. In eighteen cases, viewing time was limited to two hours daily and the symptoms faded away in five or six weeks. In the eleven cases where the rules were relaxed after the initial period, the children watched as much as before and the previous symptoms returned.[6]

To test the hypothesis that such symptoms were caused by television radiation, Ott put six pots – each containing three bean seeds – in front of a colour television screen half covered with a black photographic paper which would stop all visible light. Six pots were put in front of the other half of the screen, which was shielded with lead, whilst a control of six pots was placed fifty feet away.

After three weeks, the lead-shielded and the outdoor beans showed six inches normal growth. The beans subjected to radiation, 'showed an excessive vine-type growth ranging up to 31 1/2 inches. Furthermore, the leaves were all approximately 2 1/2 to 3 times the size of those of the outdoor plants and those protected by the lead shielding.'

A similar experiment was done on rats. The rats shielded by black paper alone, 'became increasingly hyperactive and aggressive within from three to ten days, and then became progressively lethargic. At thirty days they were extremely lethargic and it was necessary to push them to make them move about the cage'. Those rats behind the lead shielding showed much milder abnormal symptoms, which also took much longer to develop.[7]

Perhaps the most important work of Ott in this context was on fluorescent light, since television is fluorescent. He discovered that different forms of light had marked effects on 'the streaming of the chloroplasts' — the forming movement of cells within plants. Whilst subjected to sunlight a rhythmical pattern would be maintained, but with different fluorescents the pattern changed dramatically.

The next step was to subject cancer-sensitive mice to different lights. An experiment with 300 such mice showed a 61% survival rate with pink fluorescent, 94% with white fluorescent, 88% with all fluorescents and 97% for ordinary daylight.

On the basis of Ott's research, Jerry Mander reasons that if people are watching television for four hours per day they, 'are soaking up far more television light, directed straight into their eyes, than any kind of artificial light that preceded it.'[8]

Mander observes that on the colour television screen there are myriads of red, blue and green dots or lines. These phospors glow when shot at by the cathode gun and the viewer combines the dots into coloured images. This is in effect fluorescent light. From Ott's researches, especially the red fluorescent in television could have harmful effects, particularly on sensitive babies and young children.

Whilst the effects of light on natal jaundice and rickets are widely known, there is little experimental evidence about the effects of television light on people. Dr. Richard J. Wurtman, a professor of endocrinology and metabolism at the Massachusetts Institute of Technology, wrote a paper in the *Scientific American* on the effects of artificial light. Whilst agreeing with Ott that the body may be radically influenced by different light spectra, Wurtman concludes ominously: —

Both government and industry have been satisfied to allow people who buy electric lamps — first the incandescent ones and now the fluorescent — to serve as the unwitting subjects in a long-term experiment on the effects of artificial lighting environment on human health. We have been lucky, perhaps, in that so far the experiment has had no demonstrably baneful effects.

## *Is Television light harmful to children's health?*

Scientists such as Wurtman and Ott are agreed on the following points: —

Light coming through the eyes and skin has concrete, biochemical effects on the body, and provides nourishment. As evidenced by the changes in cellular activity, different types of light have various effects on the human organism. Apart from helping synthesize Vitamin D and overcoming infantile jaundice, not much is yet known about these effects. Ingesting television light affects our organism, especially the red fluorescent in colour television according to Ott. Ott also observed that the television phospors have 'narrow wavelength peaks, just as in fluorescent', which might be risky because of the absorption of a large concentration of light within one spectral range.[10]

Since babies and children are so sensitive to light that it is a biological need, then, until the effects of television light are more deeply researched, it might be safer to restrict viewing. Certainly for babies and toddlers there is no better light diet than daylight or sunlight, even though artificial light is unavoidable and something to which they have to become accustomed. But let us hope that babies, who according to Leboyer have senses with 'the sharpness and freshness of absolute youth' will no longer be subjected to television light.

A further point of concern made by Ott is whether the chemical effects of X-rays on living tissues are fully known. The extremely low levels of X-rays that modern television sets give off may have effects without showing any visible damage. (Faulty sets may give off higher levels of radiation, in some cases behind the set). Ott observes that the upward-growing bean roots looked normal, as did the aggressive rats. He asks whether the low permitted levels of radiation may affect the behaviour and learning of children without exhibiting physical damage.

Finally, Ott makes a controversial point in concluding his chapter on the 'T.V. Radiation Story': —

> I am constantly asked what is a safe distance for children to watch when watching T.V., but when I think of the rat breeding colony being so completely disrupted at a distance of fifteen feet with two intervening building partitions, I can only answer that I really don't know, but that the distance that might be considered safe would undoubtedly vary with different sets.[11]

## *Postscript : T.V. radiation*

Ott's work triggered a huge debate in the late 1960's on T.V. Radiation. T.V. sets were discovered which emitted radiation at many times the "safe" level of 0.5 millirems per hour. Since 1946 T.V.set manufacturers had been aware their sets produced low level radiation, but from 1946—1962, there was no published material to inform the viewing public of the fact. Otts work blew the whistle in 1966.

One set manufacturer, General Electric, found in 1966 that there were significant levels of ionizing radiation being emitted by its colour T.V. sets. These levels were one hundred thousand times, higher than the recommended standard of 0.50 millirems, per hour. The company did not inform consumers, but identified the cause of the excessive radiation, and in April 1967 began locating and repairing the 154,000 defective sets. Informing consumers would have caused "unfounded fears", i.e. that they were receiving on average ten times the current yearly exposure of nuclear industry workers. One wonders what General Electric would have called "founded fears".

Joyce Nelson, who raises this issue in *The Perfect Machine*, describes how the US National Center for Radiological Health tried to calm public fears.[12] The industry tried to claim these T.V. Radiation problems were an isolated case. But Ott's research pointed to the electronic medium itself. By January 1968, President Johnson in his state of the Union Message called for "protection against hazardous radiation from television sets and other electronic equipment." Surveys of sets made by different manufacturers highlighted radiation problems with a significant proportion. The US Surgeon General then warned T.V. viewers to sit from 6ft to 10ft from their sets, but with no reason given why this distance was "safe". Survey findings discovered radiation behind and beside sets. One estimate assumed that 800,000 households had sets emitting radiation over the "safe limits". In April 1969, the Public Health Service of Suffolk County, New York found that 20% of colour sets (one thousand out of the sample of five thousand) were emitting radiation in excess of 0.5 mr/hr. Repair men had boosted the picture tube voltage to get clearer T.V. pictures in areas with poor reception which interfered with radiation containment devices. Proposals to limit set emission to 0.1 mr/hr were defeated in Congress — the level of 0.5 mr/hr was legislated for. Ralph Nader reacted : —

The standards are too low. Millions of people are being exposed to the risk of physical, genetic and eye damage... The forces of industry and bureaucracy have prevailed.

With the advent of solid-state components in the early 1970's a technology which it is believed solves the radiation problem, the old T.V. technology was phased out. Legislation, and the new technology, had solved the problem. However, as late as 1976, John Ott continued to refer to "radiation from T.V. picture tubes" in his book *Health & Light*. There has been much research and debate about the effects of the Visual Display Units or Terminals used by microcomputers which is discussed in Appendix I.

## Conclusion : more research needed

The effects of light and low level radiation on health need much further research before firm conclusions can be made. Ott's experiments were made in the mid 1960's with T.V. sets using a different technology from the solid state components used now.

However, the fact that Dr Rosaline Bertell's findings on the effects of low level radiation and John Ott's work on light and health have not been systematically followed up, is of concern. [13]

# Chapter Seven

## *Television as teacher*

*"... television is the prime educator in the world today. It is the school's primary competitor for children's minds."*

*Jim Trelease.[1]*

*"...the major educational enterprise now being undertaken in the United States is not happening in its classrooms but in the home, in front of the television set, and under the jurisdiction not of school administrators and teachers but of network executives and entertainers. I don't mean to imply that the situation is a result of a conspiracy or even that those who control television want this responsibility. I mean only to say that, like the alphabet or the printing process, television has by its power to control the time, attention and cognitive habits of our youth, gained the power to control their education."*

*Neil Postman [2]*

### 'T.V. is educational'

This is the tail end of most conversations about whether television is really a necessity in the home. People, after running down the programme content, admitting that they fall asleep in front of the box, often say 'they don't know why they keep the thing' – but if you ask why they still do so then the little tag comes out 'but it's so educational for the children'.

Many children spend more time watching television than they do in school. Since television has become a major educational influence, it is legitimate to ask, 'What are the effects of television on children's education.' We need to explore the effects of television on speech, language, imagination, comprehension, play, attention and moral development – not just the well-known effects such as increasing general knowledge.

The television as teacher is an issue for both parents and school. Some playgroups, kindergartens and Steiner or Waldorf schools actively discourage viewing at home, and try to suggest alternative activities. Some teachers use television carefully with older children and teenagers for particular purposes. However, few people have come to terms with Jim Trelease' thesis that T.V. is the school's primary competitor for children's minds, or with Neil Postman, that television is turning education into an amusing activity. In fact, it is hard to imagine home or school life without television.

## School life without television

It is hard to imagine a life without television, so ingrained has it become in our way of life. Indeed, the small minority of people without sets are often harassed by post office inspectors who cannot believe they lack the box! It is harder to come across teachers whose experience embraces pre-television days. One teacher, however, with eight years experience in Britain, gave a vivid description of school and community life without television in Malta in 1978:—

> Since teaching here I have been impressed by the high standard of education the children receive. Malta has a television service which rarely begins before 6.30 p.m., with children's programmes which last for an hour. The programmes are then all in Maltese until approximately 9 p.m. I have found with the lack of available English speaking programmes the children have developed their interests away from television. They read many, many books, both 'readers' and library books. At times, it is difficult to keep up with hearing everybody read every day, although we are helped in this by having relatively small classes. The children also join clubs such as cubs and brownies, adventure groups and partake in sporting activities... However, after eight years of teaching in the U.K. I am singularly impressed by the children here in Malta who literally beg for homework, and do it with lots of interested help from parents. I have also noticed that the children's news never carries reports of television programmes but of excursions and activities carried out over the weekend with parents and friends .[3]

Even though the special circumstances of a service school — in an expatriate community and in a country full of opportunities for outdoor pastimes — might account for such a central interest in education, this is a vivid picture of life without television. I know from my son's school, which has a policy of informing parents about the developmental consequences for children watching television, that children are highly motivated to learn and that parents are involved in many supportive activities. (Too many, I think sometimes!)

But I remember the class of forty four eleven year olds I taught once in Brighton, who watched on average over thirty hours a week. What educational effects was it having on them? Like the teacher in Malta, I often thought how much more the children might get out of school without the television as teacher as home. But these are subjective speculations; let us now turn to what research has been done on the educational effects of television.

## No harm or benefit from viewing? Early research in the 1950's

When television as a nationwide service was first introduced in the 1950's, the Nuffield Foundation funded research into the impact of television on children. A four-year study. *Television and the Child* showed that from an empirical view, based on statistics, it cannot be shown that normal, healthy, intelligent and well-adjusted children from stable families and friends — either suffer harm *or* benefit from viewing to any significant extent. [4]

This survey highlighted several points. Normal children do not benefit or suffer significantly from viewing. They spend more time watching than any other single leisure activity. Viewing soon becomes a habit and a routine, and the appeal lay in its easy availability and its value as a time-filler.

Several observations can be made on the basis of this survey. The children (10–11 and 13–14 year-olds) were not subjected to television in their pre-school days since broadcasts only became widespread on both BBC and ITV channels in the mid-1950s at the time of the survey (1954–1958). Hence their early development was not affected by television, and being normal healthy children, television viewing at a later stage seemed neither to have a positive nor a negative effect. But now that children watch on average at least twenty hours per week, the effects might by very different. Secondly, the fact that the Nuffield children used television as a time-filler, on average 11–13 hours per week, a whole waking day or a large proportion of their free time — is significant. Television is a voracious thief of time, and the question here is how much more beneficial alternative hobbies, such as sports, play, social and family activities might have been, than viewing. Thirdly, the report pointed even then to the dangers of television to handicapped and less able children:—

> How much a child views depends mainly on how intelligent he is: more addicts are to be found among average and duller children than among brighter ones.
>
> It was found that the confirmed addict is not an only child but an insecure one, who finds relationships with other children difficult and who seeks companionship and security in television and other mass media.
>
> The addict has less desire to do things for himself and is more often prepared to see things on television rather than in real life.[4]

Since 1958, divorce rates have climbed to one in three marriages and stable family life has been eroded as a consequence. The number of children who are maladjusted, hyperactive or who have some social and learning difficulties has risen. From the report's findings, therefore, such children are more likely to become T.V. addicts, even if viewing excessively is not a cause of their social and learning problems. Furthermore, whilst the children of intelligence do not suffer harm (or benefit) from viewing, the less able might:

> In general, it seems, the groups most influenced are children from secondary modern school, especially those of only average and dull— average intelligence.[4]

Simply put, therefore, the report implies that television viewing may widen the educational gap between the more able and the less able.

The question parents ask most often is how viewing affects the ability to read, and literacy. There has been a great deal of research and discussion of this question, since viewing has displaced reading as children's most popular leisure time activity.

## Television and literacy

'*Literacy is out — video literacy is in*': Guardian Businessman of the Year.

Evidence about declining standards of literacy has been accumulating over the last few years. Since 1964, children's reading skills have been declining. According to the National Foundation for Educational Research, the eleven year old of 1971 was four months behind his 1964 peer in reading ability.

This complements popular views, whether in fact true or not, that there are declining standards in our schools. The young do not read much, for example, over a quarter of sixteen year olds do not read books outside school — whilst for most of them the most popular leisure activity is television.

Coincidentally, by 1964 over 90% of homes had a television set and most children had begun to watch from an early age. Leading educationalists began to ask if there was a link between viewing and declining reading efficiency.

Lady Plowden wrote to *The Times* on the publication of the N.F.E.R. report: —

Learning to read is not sufficient; the skill must be practised. The book in easy language finds it hard to compete with the sophistication and the excitement of television. Stories about little Eskimo or Indian children are poor fare compared with *Doctor Who* [5]

The transition from children reading before bedtime, or being read a story by parents, or seeing their own parents read — to watching television, may account for the decline in 'the reading habit'. For parents and teachers encouraging regular reading-habits in children, it seems now a battle between the box and the printed word. [5]

In the U.S.A 1964 was a turning point for literacy levels also, because since then there has been a steady decline in college entrance examination scores. In 1977 the College Entrance Board published a report *On Further Examination* on the causes of the decline. [5]

The report mentions that by sixteen, most children have watched television for 10,000—15,000 hours, or more time than they spent in school. At six years, the average viewing time is 20—35 hours per week, peaking at twelve years. Between 1960 and 1970 the viewing time per day increased by roughly an hour.

The authors believe television is *a* cause of declining literacy levels, and, although they cannot prove it, they observe that: 'Television has become a surrogate parent, substitute teacher'. They say that television is a thief of students' time, and that teachers' performance cannot compete with T.V. stars 'who can sing and dance while they add and subtract and do the alphabet.'

Secondly, they questioned whether the T.V./brain phenomenon was a cause ie the tuning out of the logical, verbal left brain when viewing:[1]

> Could this much (10,000 to 15,000 hours) functioning of one area of the brain alter the neural mechanisms of the mind — with *possible* effect on the handling of verbal materials? [6]

Even though it is hard to single out television as a major cause of young Americans' decline in verbal abilities — changes in teaching methods and in the test population may also be causes — other factors reinforce the initial hypothesis. Firstly, scores have declined continuously since 1964 and secondly, there are increasingly fewer high scores, and more low scores, rather than an all—round decrease.

To explain these phenomena, Marie Winn relates them to the increase in set ownership since 1950. In 1950, when television became a mass medium, 4,000,000 sets were sold. By 1955, 67% of households had sets, increasing to 88% in 1960, 96% in 1970 and by 1975 virtually all homes had television (if not several sets). From these figures, the decline in verbal scores may be linked with the increasing numbers of 'television children' taking the exam, as well as the steady increase in the average number of viewing hours per child.

Furthermore, whilst television in the 1950's tended not to affect the brighter children, who watched less and read more than the less able, by 1970 viewing had overtaken reading. Their scores have declined most sharply.

In the absence of any 'national standards' of achievement, it is difficult to make such close links between viewing and the decline in verbal abilities here as is possible in the U.S.A. However, because there has been a decline in reading standards since 1964, the question of whether television is undermining literacy is vital one to ask — and to keep asking.

## *Viewing and learning to speak : 'Mum, talk to me...'*

In Birmingham, an early language project has been started in a deprived suburb to encourage mothers to talk with their babies and toddlers. The campaign was started because teachers found that the vocabulary of the children first coming to nursery school was contracting, and that they could not speak as once they used to.

Several reasons have been suggested for this, such as the replacement of terrace housing by high-rise flats, the break—up of large families, the number of single parent families, the incidence of isolated children and the lack of parents playing with babies. In addition, writes Denis Herbstein of the *Sunday Times*, 'The most pervasive toy is television. Gone are the days when mum, and especially dad read a story to his child before lights out. Now it is a dismissive peck on the cheek before Coronation Street'.[7]

Great social upheavals have not prevented the handing on of nursery rhymes between parents and children. Television — along with less significant social causes — may have almost put paid to the transmission of nursery rhymes, according to the Assistant Mistresses' association.

According to infant-teachers, nursery rhymes are of vital importance in developing the speech, language and basic numeracy of young children. Rhymes like, 'One, Two, Three, Four, Five, Once I caught a fish alive', or 'Ten Green Bottles', teach numbers, words and rhymes. They are also helpful for better physical co-ordination. Through such rhymes as 'Humpty Dumpty', and 'This is the House that Jack Built' vocabularies are widened. Children taught such family rhymes may know as many as two thousand words by the age of five, and be able to take in colour, shape and numbers. However, many children had only a vocabulary of fifty words on coming to school, which may be attributed to effects of television.

The Assistant Mistresses' working party was headed by Mrs. Pierce-Price, who described nursery rhymes as 'a foreign art'. According to members of the working party, even though nursery rhymes were on television, children failed to learn them. They thought that a reason for children not knowing nursery rhymes was because television was a 'look and forget' rather than a 'look and learn' medium.[8]

Children learn to speak through imitating, listening to and conversing with real, live people. They need to make contact with the 'genius' of language with its life, its sense and movement through other speakers. Mechanically reproduced voices on television are no substitute for real conversation. I hope the experiment will never be done, but I would venture the hypothesis that it would be impossible or very difficult, for a young child to learn to speak through the television medium alone.

As mentioned previously, television watching may blunt a commitment to language by delaying the development of the verbal areas of the brain — at a crucially 'language sensitive age'.

The importance of 'Mum, speak to me', cannot be over-emphasised. Babies first hear conversation around them, and probably understand a great deal when spoken with. In the later months they exercise their vocal organs through 'babbling', and begin to imitate words, often repeating them over and over again. Television, as opposed to a brother, sister of parent, does not wait for a response, nor does it have a smiling face or a warm hug.

Imitation, rehearsal and repetition help the toddler to master words, phrases and meanings from other people — conversation being the optimal condition for language development. Repeating rhymes like 'Little Bo Peep' or 'Pat-a-cake Baker's Man' help with clarity of speech, with getting a real feel for the language, for discovering the excitement in words and for rhythm. A child with a rich fund of nursery rhymes, songs and stories will have a head start at school.

One hospital play therapist described the pathetic case of a little boy brought in with a 'speech deficiency'. He was a T.V. addict and gun crazy, with a limited vocabulary. The commonest words he used were 'Bang! Bang!' Faith Hall recalls a boy brought to her with multiple speech difficulties and general debility. She recommended "no television" on finding him to be an 'addict', which proved in this particular case to be a cure for the problem.

Obviously, retarded verbal skills cannot be related to television alone, whether a symptom or a cause. One mother believes that the key factor may be the amount parents talk with each other, and their television habits. She wrote that:—

> The children I have known who have speech difficulty (and how incoherent a normal five year old can be) are the children of those parents who watch too much television. Consequently, conversation in these homes is minimal and the child's speech suffers because they only learn by listening and imitating. As the child gets older too much television can be harmful but the damage has already been done.

This theory can be given a graphic, if unfortunate, illustration by the following example of Faith Hall:—

> A boy of about ten was brought to the Speech clinic, with a moderately severe, repetitive stammer. During the interview with the mother, to try to determine the cause of the speech difficulty, the mother said that the father was a complete T.V. addict. Every day when the boy tried eagerly to tell his Dad about the events of his day at school or at play, the father would turn round angrily from watching television and snap at him to 'Shut up!' and not interrupt his viewing. So the boy was repeatedly cut off in mid-sentence, which had the effect of making him stammer. This had been going on for a long time, and the speech deteriorated accordingly. Asked if she thought the father would accept advice from the therapist about the desirability of changing his T.V. habits, the mother adamantly and gloomily said, 'No, he'll never change, not even to help his own son'.

Our local health visitors and speech therapists are concerned about the late acquisition of language of an increasing number of youngsters. These children come from a variety of socio-economic backgrounds, and one important factor is television. One health visitor remembered a parent describing her youngster, "He's quite an intelligent little boy — he knows how to put the video on!". During the 1 — 2 years language receptive phase, they feel T.V. is not a way of helping children acquire language. In any case because of the single focus, short attention span of toddlers, they cannot cope with the barrage of words from television. Even children's programmes such as *Playschool*, are at too high a level, are not appropriate and meaningful. "T.V. offers nothing to children under three in terms of language acquisition," said one speech therapist. Language develops from communication between people, and television does not respond to the child. T.V. ...displaces play and talking...or later, at seven or eight, watching and discussing special programmes with a parent would help stimulate language development".

## Television and reading: lazy readers?

When I was visiting a class of eight year olds at a local school, the teacher pointed out several 'lazy readers', children who could read perfectly well but who either were not interested enough to read or who found it difficult to get inside what they were reading. Such lazy readers found the necessary concentration, focusing of attention and effort hard to make; in addition, the teacher found their comprehension of what was being read was somewhat vague. Significantly, he linked this with television-viewing at home and the lack of a domestic 'reading habit'. Certain non-television children in the class read regularly at home. These latter children did very well in school.

The same pattern was revealed in teachers' letters, of non-television children having educational advantages over television children, particularly in reading.

Literacy – reading and writing – is basic to our society. People who are illiterate feel themselves to be outsiders or even stigmatized. Writing and reading are therefore important accomplishments, and any factor which may have adverse effects, such as television, needs careful study. Many teachers who wrote to Faith Hall as a result of the campaign felt themselves to be old-fashioned in having to 'stick up' for literacy in a television age.

The 'television age' in which the visual image has displaced the printed word is only just over 30 years old. Until the 'print age' when literacy finally became widespread over the last century, most cultures were oral. When I was doing social research in the Faroes, I encountered a rich oral tradition through the old people there. Far into the early hours of the morning, they would recite the ancient sagas, myths, stories and ballads of their people. In former days, children in such cultures entered the imaginative world through hearing, learning and reciting the old sagas and stories.

The relics of the oral tradition still survived into the print age for young children. Stories were told to children before bedtime, nursery rhymes and games were learned by children who explored the world of imagination, of language, poetry and music through adults. The cultivation of such rich oral culture for children was traditionally acknowledged by 'common sense' and by teachers as a sound pre-school preparation for literacy.

Now, however, it is television which dominates the pre-school culture of children – and which has displaced much reading from school-age children's lives. Instead of encountering stories, through another person with whom they can explore the world in the case of pre-school children, or being able to imagine for themselves the stories they read, children are meeting the world through television, mostly without adults to help them.

Many people will somehow feel that reading is 'better' than viewing for children. To compare the nature of the two media may be instructive in this respect. Reading necessitates concentration, focusing, thought, imagination and the ability to have 'inner vision', to visualise. Television requires little concentration, de-focuses the mind, lames the capacity for visualisation by the substitution of electronically produced images, and encourages passivity. A reader can vary the pace, or even put down a book if it becomes too exciting, whereas television controls the pace and because of its addictive, hypnotic effects, makes it very difficult for children to switch off. The reader is in charge of the book, but the television is usually in control of the viewer. Reading a book allows one to create one's own unique pictures of events and people, at one's own pace, and encourages a more profound understanding. Television imposes the same standard interpretation of a novel, such as *The Secret Garden* for millions of viewers. The same people reading the book would have created millions of different versions of it. Furthermore, whilst children who read can also write, and hence understand the medium they are using, very few young children understand the television world and how it works.

Since the above comparisons may be dismissed as 'common sense' — research into brain-wave patterns backs up the differences mentioned above between television and print.

Herbert Krugman, in experimenting with the electrical responses of the brain to print and television, arrived at results which confirm common sense. There was 'a picture of relaxed attention, interest and mental activity' in response to reading. The television response was 'a relaxed condition with elements of both drowsiness and alertness' which also showed signs of boredom.[9]

The high frequency of alpha waves recorded in viewers does not occur normally when the eyes are open. Alpha are slow synchronous waves with no function, and usually appear when the eyes are shut. When the eyes open, the brain is supposed to attend to what you are seeing, and alpha normally disappears. People who watch television may tend to fall into alpha during the visual state — as if staring at a blank visual field.

This research was confirmed by psycho-physiologist Thomas Mulholland, and Peter Crown (a professor of television and psychology at Hampshire College, Massachusetts), who connected electrodes to the heads of both adult and child viewers. The researchers believed beforehand that the children viewing exciting programmes would show patterns of high attention. In other words, they would react to the content of the show. He was surprised by the results which showed exactly the reverse. Viewers showed greatly increased alpha waves, indicating passivity, as if they were 'just sitting quietly in the dark'.[10]

To summarise, when reading, one is attentive, aware of one's awareness, in control of the pace of the book and actively engaged in re-creating the story. When viewing, one is distracted, barely conscious, in the control of the television and passively receiving images in an automatic way. Not only is the implication of Mulholland's work that television is a training course in inattention, but that whilst viewing, the self, one's 'I', is barely present as an active centre of one's thoughts, feelings and actions. One is 'spaced out' of one's mind, one's conscious self is temporarily absent, leaving the television to imprint its images subconsciously on an open mind and organism.

In fact, viewing T.V. is a totally different experience from reading. Television trains short attention spans. Reading stimulates long attention spans, books are written to keep children's attention – not to grab it and constantly interrupt it. T.V. is full of images, fast paced action – reading involves thinking, reflection, moving at one's own pace. One can put a book down, and pick it up again.

Young children usually look at books, *with* adults or older children who read to them. Books are a social experience – you can talk about them and share them at bedtime. Television for young children is often an anti-social experience – with limited conversation, perhaps alone and passively watching. Television also gives answers all the time – children learn by asking questions.

One can argue that television can encourage the reading of certain serialised books, like *The Lion the Witch and the Wardrobe* or *The Little House in the Big Woods*. Also, that BBC's storytelling programme for young children, *Jackanory*, encourages the reading of the featured stories. These are welcome spin offs. But the fact is that television has displaced reading as most children's most popular leisure activity.

Since many parents ask me during discussions about when it is appropriate for children to start viewing, I often suggest the time *after* they have learned to enjoy reading. Until the reading habit has been firmly established, at from seven to nine years of age, viewing may undermine reading skills and enjoyment. One research finding which would back this up was that Jerome and Dorothy Singer of Yale University found that light viewers learned to read more easily than heavy viewers.

Tannis Williams study of Notel found that second graders (eight year olds) scored higher on a test of reading fluency than did the second graders in Unitel or Multitel where there was T.V. Four years later, when T.V. was available in Notel, there was no difference amongst second graders as to reading fluency. Williams concluded that viewing holds up the ability to read by using time which would otherwise be spent with books.

## How much do pre-school children understand?

An adult and a four year old watching the same programme will, because of the different stages of their cognitive development, be seeing two 'different' programmes. The pre—school child is ego-centric in his thinking, and this will colour his viewing. Grant Noble in *Children in Front of the Small Screen*, lists five ways that children's viewing may be coloured:—

> Children are likely to react in an all-or-nothing way to television. People will be 'good' or 'bad', 'ugly' or 'beautiful', 'black' or 'white' — with no consciousness of any shades of grey.
>
> Secondly, the pre-school child will only view things from his own standpoint. It is impossible to differentiate between 'inner' experiences like dreams, or 'outer' experiences like television. Television will therefore be 'real' because the child is capable of picturing that people are only acting.
>
> Thirdly, the child may believe he can affect events on the television, sees himself as involved in the programme, and places himself beside the characters.
>
> Children define objects by their location in relation to themselves. When a scene changes, and an actor reappears in a new situation, and looks larger or smaller than he did previously, he may be taken to be a completely different character from the one seen previously.

Lastly, young children cannot usually reverse operations in thought, it is difficult for them to reason, being still at a pre-conceptual stage. It is therefore difficult for them to follow a storyline on television, for they find it hard to comprehend that it has a beginning, a middle and an end.[11]

Young children, therefore, tend to be dominated by their visual field, and live fully in the 'here and now'. Given the above account of the 'pre-conceptual' stage of three and four year olds' development, how much of what they view is understood?

Studies of children's comprehension have found that they enjoy viewing programmes geared to their age, but that they understand little of the content.

In one study a fairytale was shown to children of four, seven and ten years. When their understanding was tested, only 20% of the four year olds had comprehended the story. The older ones understood far more. The conclusion was that 'pre-school children were unable to either remember what they had seen with any fidelity or to interpret accurately why the characters acted as they did.[12]

Others have interpreted this experiment in a different way. Children of this age differ from older ones since they need to hear stories repeated over and over again, and often their favourites have repetition as a theme, for example, 'This is the house that Jack Built', 'Goldilocks', and 'The Three Little Pigs'. The continual novelty and fast moving pace of television programmes cuts across this need for repetition. Only the advertisers seem to understand how effective the repetition of a jingle can be and make good use of this principle of learning.

A four year old friend, after a news programme on the 1980 British Steel strike, announced forthrightly, 'I want to be a picket when I grow up!' How many programmes do pre-school children watch, even ones made especially for them, of which they comprehend little? It is the rare parent that sits down with a young child to interpret what is happening on the screen or to repeat what happened afterwards. Most children are left alone to ingest their 20—30 hours weekly diet of television. How much do pre-school children understand? — the answers seems to be 'very little' of programmes made for adults.

## Play-deprivation

A child's work is her play, this involves imitation, re-creation, invention, creation and imagination. Through play, a young child first imitates the everyday happenings in the world of his home and neighbourhood, and then re-creates them dramatically, Play is the gateway to the imagination, but also to acquiring social skills, co-ordination, and an understanding of the world. 'Let's play daddies and mummies, doctors and patients, shopkeepers, going on holidays...' is an invitation to be active, to explore, to have fun and to imagine.

Limited opportunities to play, for example no local outdoor play facilities, no playmates, toys that are so 'perfect' (i.e. highly finished) they leave nothing to the imagination, and little parental encouragement may cause play deprivation. Television, of course, steals vast amounts of time from the serious work of young children's play. (This is not to mention the estimated annual £1 billion spent on running the television network and over £3,000 million tied up in television sets – a fraction of which could be well spent on play facilities!)

'All Jim can use sticks for is guns! He can't imagine them being brooms, spades, spoons, wands or feathers like the non-television children,' a nursery teacher called John commented to me. He continued, 'There were three children playing with a chest of wooden blocks. One (not a viewer) was thoroughly absorbed – it was amazing what came out of him! You could see the difference between him, and another boy of five with a high exposure to television. He borrowed ideas and found it hard to play with much inventiveness.'

In some nursery schools I know, where teachers carefully observe the ability to play of new children, such observations were confirmed. Teachers generally observe that heavy viewers typically are less imaginative and less dramatic in their play, show less initiative, are more likely to expect to be entertained, can pay less attention to stories, sometimes lack co-ordination and do not play so constructively as non-viewing children. Non-viewers, such teachers believe, behave much more like children of thirty years ago.

It may take several months, if not two years, to make up for the play deprivation that may have partly resulted from television. One remedial teacher from Essex wrote that:. . .Very young children who watch television extensively are missing tactile concrete experiences vital to motor development, and hand-eye co-ordination. Should a child miss nursery education, the first few weeks in the infant school could well be the first attempt at 'writing'. The teacher has then to find time and opportunity to go through the 1½ year plus stages of scribbling, and drawing. A child could well be disadvantaged by 2½–3 years before arriving at the infant school. A sobering thought!

## Creativity and imagination

Tannis Williams found that in Notel, the introduction of television affected the performance of adults of creative problem solving tasks. The tasks required thinking of less likely alternatives to the problem, and not getting bogged down in the "obvious" approaches. Adults from Notel solved the problems faster than did the adults from the T.V. town – and the unsuccessful persisted longer.

The conclusions were that television may lead to "decreased attention and/a tolerance of frustration". The displacement of problem solving experiences by viewing, may result in a more limited repertoire of divergent solutions.

What, however, are the effects of viewing on young children's creativity and imagination? Tim Hicks, in a paper on toys, is concerned that the fresh, lively, imaginative receptivity of children is being exploited by the television medium. He writes:

> With television, the manufacturers had direct access to the image receptive consciousness of children. Children are by nature ready for, needing and unconsciously seeking the images that teach them what the world is and who they are. They look out to discover the world and everything that comes to them adds to their ongoing definition. Being thus growing and forming themselves and their understanding of the world, they are deeply vulnerable to the influence of the images presented on television and become captured by the images. Television is such a powerful manipulating and influencing factor because it places images directly into the consciousness of the child in an almost surgical fashion with the child having almost no barriers with which to protect him or herself. [14]

Our children's imaginations are co-opted by the penetrating images of the toy manufacturers. Children lose the internal space to create their own images and begin to be able to envision and structure their own emerging experience only in the images delivered so persistently by the mass marketeers.

Television has begun a process which may lead to the rigidifying of the imagination, and instead of developing one's own imaginative powers as a child, one will merely develop the ability to manipulate images on the screen. Video graphics enable children to make images on the television screen. One advertisement read: —

> Nothing is as mesmerising to kids as television. Nothing commands so much of their attention or occupies so much of their time . . . In the beginning it (i.e. T.V.) controlled them."
>   With the video graphics software, children will now be able, ". . . to take complete control over the television. To light up the screen with their own images."

The dangers of television and computer graphics to the development of the imagination and creativity are great. However, viewed positively, the onus is on parents and teachers to bring up their children so creatively that not only do they develop lively imaginations, but that they are immune to television's fixed imagery. I remember our children visiting another family, where Laura Ingalls Wilder's *Little House in the Big Woods* was on television. "That's nothing like the real story", said one son, and went away to play.


## Sleep deprivation

Instead of meeting a lively class of children refreshed from sleep, (many) teachers see many of their pupils come to school tired, from watching television late. One primary teacher wrote: —

> The biggest television influence was one of general tiredness. I would estimate that 90% of the children come to school tired, i.e. with bags under their eyes. I found that children went to sleep in class many times because they were tired.

A teacher with pre-television experience commented how easy it is to observe which children have watched television the night before. He said, "Their eyes lack lustre, their breathing is shallow and their posture reminds one of a set of documents held together by a perished rubber band."
  Furthermore, this teacher described the 'Monday morning syndrome': —

> Not only is there the deadening effect on children's will activity, but to achieve a good lesson on a Monday morning the teacher

must devote at least the first half hour to movement in all its forms − P.E., movement exercises, recitation of poems, the tables and singing.

One survey showed that about twenty five per cent of five to eight year olds are still watching at nine o'clock in the evening, whilst half the nine to eleven year olds are watching after nine.[13] An earlier BBC audience research survey showed that the figures for viewing between 9.00 p.m. and 9.30 p.m.. are:−

| Children aged | 5 − 7 | 8 − 11 | 12 − 14 |
|---|---|---|---|
| | 7% | 27% | 51% |

The PYE report showed that 45% of children aged seven to ten stay up until 9.00 p.m. to watch television, and a further 9% until 10.00 p.m.

The widespread reports by teachers of the majority of their pupils who come to school tired and glassy−eyed, are therefore reinforced by these startling figures. Several teachers have remarked to me how their pupils showed a great increase in alertness during the 1973 'three day week', when television shut down at ten o'clock.

Adequate sleep is vital to children's healthy development, and as the old saying observes, 'Early to bed, early to rise, makes a man healthy, wealthy and wise', (My wife always adds 'socially unacceptable!').

A good sleep is the prerequisite for a good day at school, sleep helps to build up the growing organism, and also, through dreaming, enables us to re-work the day's experiences imaginatively so as to integrate them and become free of them. Dreaming is both a psychological and biological necessity.

But dreams after television may be disturbed for children. The vivid images resurface and are the cause of many nightmares. One mother recounted how her youngest daughter had her first nightmare after seeing Dr. Who, without her parents' knowledge.

Dr. Edelston, a child psychiatrist and the original director of the Bradford Child Guidance Clinic, wrote in Community Health:−

Now there is one very clear effect of T.V. viewing which we come across with increasing frequency in children referred to us at the School Psychological Clinic in Bradford, more and more of them, in recent years, are troubled with nightmares with the content derived from television characters.

Such nightmares are experienced in about half the children examined and their content depends on the current programmes. Dr. Edelston observed that in 1978, in '...the last year or so, Dracula is by far the commonest frightening figure, with Frankenstein, Dr. Who and derivatives, coming second.' Furthermore, the parents know little of their children's nightmares, or that they suffer from bad dreams, and are startled when shown their children's drawings.[15]

The importance of stories for the development of children's imagination and indeed their psychological growth cannot be over-emphasised. The traditional wisdom behind children being told stories at bedtime is profound. Folk tales, the nursery stories of the 'Three Pigs' or the 'White Pet' and Grimm's fairy tales — told by a real person — are treasure houses of archetypes and images, which once planted in a child's sensitive imagination continue to work in a therapeutic way throughout life. The archetypes of the king, the princess, the huntsman, or the wise old woman — are 'unfinished' images which can be forever reworked through dreams.

Television images are ready made, fixed and static with little inherent capacity for transformation. These images are imprinted on the child's mind, *in a process which by-passes consciousness.* They enter the child's psyche like stones, as opposed to the infinitely malleable images re-created by a child from stories told to them. Whereas television images are 'junk food for dreaming', fairy stories are the real stuff.

Bruno Bettelheim, in *'The Uses of Enchantment — The Meaning and Importance of Fairy Tales'*, writes that:–

> Each fairy tale is a magic mirror which reflects some aspects of our inner world, and of the steps required by our evolution from immaturity to maturity. For those who immerse themselves in what the fairy tale has to communicate, it becomes a deep, quiet pool which at first seems to reflect only our own image, but behind it we soon discover the inner turmoils of our soul — its depth, and ways to gain peace within ourselves and with the world, which is the reward of our struggles.[16]

The 'true' fairy stories, according to Bettelheim, are those which are most helpful to the child's path of discovering meaning in life.

It is difficult to encourage parents to send their children to bed earlier, to cut down on viewing hours and to tell bedtime stories as an alternative. Teachers find it difficult to mention such things to parents because it smacks of interference in their private lives, and may harm otherwise good relationships. According to 'The Liverpool Echo' one infant school head, on being shocked to discover her pupils late viewing habits, had written to parents. She only received one reply. One of her teachers told the 'Echo': 'The mothers always lie at first when I ask them how long they allow their kids to watch. And when I persist in quizzing them about it, they just shake their heads and say they don't know'. [17]

The problem is a difficult one. But when the lack of a good night's sleep affects children's education adversely, when sleeplessness, nerves, and bad dreams are so prevalent amongst a large proportion of child viewers, it is time that television-induced 'sleep and dream deprivation' was widely recognised.

## Breakfast television and alertness

The advent of breakfast television in Britain has compounded the sleep problem mentioned above. Young viewers who are exposed to the medium whilst getting up and having breakfast, may well show signs of sleepiness, lack of alertness and fatigue during the school morning. Moreover, since one is still only half awake in the early morning, T.V. advertisers find it a very effective slot for commercials.

## 'Seeing is believing' : television and reality

Many adults believe what they see on television is an actual happening, as is shown by the floods of presents sent after a Coronation Street wedding. With three and four year olds it is difficult to help them understand television is only make–believe. One mother wrote of, '...a continual battle (with her daughter) to make her see that things shown on television were not necessarily true'. Since television channels the public's perception of social reality, moulds our consciousness — all television is, in this sense, "educational" — it is therefore vital to ask if the medium is distorting our social perceptions.

Some teachers believe television is distorting children's sense for fact or fiction. 'Docu-dramas' such as The China Syndrome', The

Bermuda Triangle or even *Holocaust*, often fail to distinguish clearly between real events and fiction. One teacher spoke of the inaccurate portrayal of human consciousness in earlier historical times, how many pupils had the impression that anything worth knowing about can be seen on the box if they watch it for long enough, and how especially in history and in science he had to break through the reality 'barrier' of 'we have seen it all on T.V.'.

An educational task of parents and teachers is to help children to grow into the social world, to come to grips with life and develop an accurate picture of social reality. The picture that heavy viewers have of social reality may be inaccurate, as surveys have shown.

Professors Larry Gross and George Gerbner of the University of Pennsylvania have researched the distorting effects of television. The results were that light viewers answered questions about the 'real world' far more accurately than heavy viewers. For example, heavy viewers consistently estimated between a 50−1 and 10−1 likelihood of meeting violence in a given week, whereas light viewers correctly estimated a 100−1 chance. Heavy viewers overestimated the population of the U.S.A. and the percentages of people working as professionals, athletes and entertainers. Subjects who had undergone higher education fared just as badly as school leavers.[18]

Such distorted perceptions of reality do not so much stem from news or documentaries, as from the repetitive programming of fiction in an apparently true-to-life way. Idealised life-styles of commercials and realistic fiction programmes slowly become incorporated in heavy viewers' 'map' of the social world.

If it is hard for college-educated adults to avoid having their perception of social reality distorted, it may be well-nigh impossible to prevent children picking up inaccurate views of the world from television.

A 1979 survey by the New York Foundation for Child Development found that children who were heavy viewers were more fearful of the world, with more nightmares, than light viewers. Another 1979 study by the Annenberg School of Communication, found that school aged children who were average viewers were more mistrustful and had an exaggerated sense of danger, compared with light viewers.

The television news is very confusing for young children to comprehend. Commercials are also difficult for infants to handle. Research conclusions about young children and advertising include the points that:−

Many young children are unable to distinguish T.V. commercials from programmes. Many children think all commercials are true. Many children do not understand the functions and techniques of advertising. Older children (nine upwards) become cynical about advertising — and that deception, misrepresentation, exaggeration and manipulation may be seen as underlying themes in the T.V. advertising world. [19]

One survey of what children watched found that *Neighbours* came in the first five places, followed by children's television programmes such as *Grange Hill* and *Blue Peter*. It is interesting to observe what picture of the world programmes such as *Neighbours* give, and to ask how healthy this picture is. For example, deceptive and simplistic thinking about complex human problems may be put over. Commercials often imply that there is a quick, easy fix for everything — a pill, spray, detergent or gadget.

The reality portrayed by good television can also be misleading. One may see a wonderful nature film, which in the space of half an hour documents the lives of some African elephants. All the highlights are shown, especially the dramatic events. The fact that hours of film, and three years' work have gone into the half hour film, may be overlooked. Everyday reality, even a safari park or zoo, just cannot compete.

To conclude, the 'sense of reality' conveyed by television may be misleading for young children. They are not at a stage of development at which they can readily distinguish fact from fiction in the way that older children can. Apart from certain specially made children's programmes, the "adult world" portrayed by television is often distorted and needs much explanation.

## Television and children with handicaps

Since television has adverse effects on children, it may have more serious effects on children with handicaps, maladjustment, and social difficulties.

In looking at television's effect on children with handicaps, it is helpful to recall that their reactions could be those of 'normal' children magnified and writ large. For example, the state of mind into which television puts habitual viewers has often been called 'T.V.

autism'. Autistic children are described as 'contact disturbed', they find it hard to make contact with people, and with themselves as an 'I', as a 'self' facing the world. We may all be 'autistic' in a small way in certain situations.

Friends of ours have two handicapped adults as loved members of their family. They got rid of their television after seeing how 'high', how 'out' of themselves, excited and obsessive it made their friends. 'If T.V. makes them high, what will it do to our young children?' the parents asked.

The use of television to drug handicapped and disturbed children is well known. E.D.Glynn reports:

> The staff of a hospital for schizophrenic adolescent girls finds that these girls, insatiable in their demands and yet themselves incapable of sustaining activity, want nothing so much as to be allowed endless hours of television. Without it they are soon noisy, unruly and frequently destructive. Significantly, the only other control these girls accept is an adult who constantly directs them or organises their entertainment for them.
>
> He adds later that: Television...is used certainly in every hospital and in every institution as an extremely effective non-chemical sedative.[20]

One educational video company recently advertised its wares with the slogan "Keep your pupils happy, let them watch a video."

Dr. Thomas Weihs, a child psychiatrist of the Camphill Rudolf Steiner Schools for Children in Need of Special Care, underlines the temptation of television for families with handicapped children. Viewing can provide comfort and relief for a hard-pressed family, as the '...one family activity in which the handicapped child can join without causing any effort on the part of the rest of the family'.[20]

Insecure children are the ones liable to become tele-addicts for they find relationships with other children difficult and discover a secure escape world in television. Insecure, withdrawn children are most likely to be adversely influenced. Whereas normal, healthy adjusted children may appear to be relatively uninfluenced by viewing, handicapped children are more vulnerable because of their more limited abilities and social skills.

Dr. Weihs cites several examples from his Camphill experiences of the effects of viewing on handicapped children. Camphill is a boarding school where there are no television sets: —

A rather forward mongol boy of fifteen years who had made very good progress for a number of years at our school, set fire to one of the outhouses on return from his summer holiday. When questioned, the boy, who was exceptionally reasonable and mature for a mongol, told us that he had seen a play on television in which a man had set fire to a house, and described the scene rather vividly. He appeared so profoundly impressed that for some time he was quite unable to arrive at any appreciation of his own action and its possible consequences in the world of realities.

A newly-admitted severely retarded post-encephalitic boy of ten years appeared to have a relatively good vocabulary and diction. As most of our staff are non-viewers, it was not realised for some time that the child's rather stereotyped phrases were acquired from television performances and that his conversation was purely a repetition of programme dialogues.

A very charming hyperkinetic (very restless) boy of eight years was admitted to one of our schools as a day-pupil. He had been a television addict for some time, viewing until late in the evening, arriving at school in the mornings exhausted, and in spite of his lively temperament unable to participate actively in class.

Even though this boy's parents stopped his viewing, he could still remember programmes in detail a month later. Dr. Weihs also mentions the 'beginning of term syndrome' in a class which was normally alert and interested, who were now, 'pre-occupied and dreamy' to an extreme extent – so that their participation could in no way be aroused. When asked what they were thinking of, their reply was 'Television'. [19]

Dr. Weihs argues that television, 'fosters immature attitudes of dependence, and easy satisfaction rather than the mature reactions of choice, decisions and effort'. As a medium, it is likely to endanger the healthy development of handicapped children. It is a worthwhile sacrifice for families not to expose their children to viewing, and he argues that this is 'in the interest of the better development and adjustment of the child in need of special care'.

This question is explored in *To a Different Drumbeat, – A practical guide to parenting children with special needs*, by Paddy Clarke, Jenny Laurnol and Holly Kofsky. [21]

Children needing remedial help are also at risk from television, according to remedial teachers. One teacher conducted a mini-survey of the seventy-five children for whom she is responsible. Their abilities vary over a wide range. Some are only slightly behind, whilst others are very backward or even mentally retarded. The teacher's observations were confined to reading, writing and verbal skills. She found that: —

1. Children who watch television extensively do not concentrate on written work as well as others.
2. Children who watch television extensively do not involve themselves in reading, or in a book as well as others.
3. Children who watch television extensively do not verbalise with their peers, or with their teachers as much, although their written work is slightly better.
4. Children who watch television moderately do gain general knowledge, and seem to have general average attainments.
5. Children who do not watch television at all (or less than an hour a week), are more keen to read and write, or verbalise more with the teacher. However, they appear to lose on general knowledge.

Whether or not such findings merely reflect the fact that non-television families may be more educationally supportive to children than television families, is difficult to find out. This teacher's survey, 'subjective' as it is, does however confirm Nuffield.

## Teaching consumerism. work, buy, consume, die

I recently saw some graffiti — 'Work, buy, consume, die', scrawled on a Bristol underpass. The task of educating people to become consumers must be one of television's most effective functions. Commercial television teaches consumerism explicitly, of course, but whether one is watching BBC or ITV one is encountering a medium which by its nature educates one passively to consume its products. One merely sits and is fed by the medium.

Good teachers have viewed television as a challenge, stimulating them to ever greater efforts to give interesting and motivating lessons. They try to use the content of programmes as a springboard for wider learning. However, many feel on the defensive against the television-dominated 'mass culture' of children. Whilst schools have to continue to teach 'the basics' to require effort from pupils and to motivate them, television offers a packaged culture of clothes, junk food, music, jingles, advertising, jargon and ready—made education. Teachers are expected to 'sell their knowledge', to 'present' lessons, to 'package' learning, to 'entertain' their pupils as if they were the 'producers' of education and their children the 'consumers'. They feel their schools are becoming like educational supermarkets, with courses, books, curricula and methods increasingly moulded by television.

Peter Abbs, an education lecturer at Sussex University, describes in *Tract* how children are not only educated by the television experience itself to be consumers, but how advertisers consciously turn toddlers into consumers.

He believes that a main aim of advertisers is to break down the mind's associative structures and insert the prefabricated frames of reference of television advertising. Just as the Jesuits were reputed to have said 'Allow me to educate a child until seven and we will convert him for life', so advertisers aim to imprint on children's minds key images, patterns, values and words before they can even speak, let alone go to school. Advertising copy-writers may express their aims like this: —

> With television we began to sell our product before they (the children) could talk. They know who the T.V. characters are before they can say full sentences.
>
> Children love their heroes, and if a hero says, 'Eat Wheaties', they will — for years and years and years. To be able to capitalise on a fad, a company has to be able to move in and out fast.
>
> If you want to create your own hard-hitting spokesman to children, the most effective way is the super-hero-miracle worker. ...A child must be able to mimic his hero, whether he is James Bond, Superman or Dick Tracy: to be able to fight and shoot without punishment or guilt feelings. [22]

Over the years, the advertisers have 'created' the teenage, teeny-bopper, weeny-bopper and now even the infant market. Many confectionery, ice-cream, music, books, records, clothes and toy companies depend on these television-created markets. Moreover, the way to adults' pockets is blazed through getting at the children first. One advertisement showed a well-heeled family in a luxury car, with a toddler in a prominent position. 'The caption read,'...and his first word was Ford'.

At Christmas time, the toy companies saturate television with advertisements. Whole ranges of programme-related books and toys are sold with 'Sesame Street' for example. Last Christmas, games like 'Intercept', 'Bombs Away! The electronic search and destroy game', or 'Stay Alive, the Ultimate Survival Game', were advertised. Such games and toys, advertised between children's programmes, sell out long before non television advertised toys.

Advertising and the medium of television itself create the child market, and keep the child consumers coming through the pipeline. Since children become what they see and imitate, and since television has the power to control our language, perception of reality and the fabric of our consciousness, advertising (as the hallmark of television) constitutes a massive intervention into children's lives and culture.

One group of American doctors has already advocated the protection of children from advertisers! In the U.S.A., according to Graham Stewart writing in the *Evening Standard*, the American Academy of Paediatrics has declared war on child advertisements. They want to protect children from the 'Gimmes', the disease of children asking for what they have seen on television advertisements. Since many children see some twenty thousand commercials a year, the doctors believe this is seriously influencing the emotional well-being of American children. Academy president Saul J. Robinson has said that the commercial exploitation of children by means of excessive, inappropriate advertising should cease. Moreover, such commercials were unfair, since young children lacked the requisite critical faculties to evaluate them objectively.[21]

There are several other reasons why young children may be adversely affected by commercials. They are fast paced, with a huge number of techniques used to rivet ones attention. The pace is overstimulating and confusing. Young children find it hard to distinguish a commercial from a programme. This ability improves with age for example over−eights could more easily see that a commercial was a commercial. Some British research found that five year olds described commercials as "showing you things to buy", but that over-eights could see that, "They're trying to sell you things".[23]

So television is a salesperson, and children who are "average viewers" may see as many as 350,000 commercials by the age of eighteen. Even though T.V. programmes like *G.I. Joe*, *Thundercats* or *Master of the Universe*, which are half-hour "toy-town" commercials, are as yet unknown in Britain, they may come with deregulation. T.V. teaches consumerism at an early age. The fast paced commercials are overstimulating, and children below eight — whilst appreciating the humour — are not normally geared up to perceive the advertising intent.

## Teaching as an amusing activity

One teacher commented to me that, 'Even if I danced naked across the desks once in a while, the pupils still wouldn't take much notice.'

Neil Postman views the two curricula of television and of school to be antagonistic. Television's message to school is that education and entertainment are the same thing. Educational T.V. is entertainment, every lesson has to be a complete package or show in itself. Television teaching should not encourage questioning, perplexity, memory, — the main aim is contentment and keeping them happy. Giving explanations, reasons, background on television is a turn-off — so everything has to be visual and dramatic. Exposition is out.

The consequence of education becoming entertainment is a,"... "massive re-orientation to learning... the refashioning of the classroom into a place where both teaching and learning are intended to be vastly amusing activities". [22]

Whatever the pros & cons of Postman's thesis, one could argue that the claims for educational television may have been exaggerated. For example, one thesis is that learning is fostered by information being dramatised, something television can do well. George Comstock reviewed 2,800 studies about television's influence on behaviour, and could not conclude that, "learning increases when information is presented in a dramatic setting." One study by Jacoby found that 3.5% of viewers could answer 12 true/false questions about two thirty second sections of commercial television programmes and advertisements. Katz found that 21 per cent of viewers were unable to recall *any* new item an hour after the broadcast. Stern found that 51% viewers were unable to recall a single news item a few minutes after viewing the T.V.news. [23]

Whilst I find that using C.C.T.V. and videos useful for teaching certain management skills like interviewing and observing non-verbal behaviour — I find that it is necessary to show short clips, point out the key issues beforehand and review afterwards. However, there are many amusing management videos on the market which entertain rather than train. Which brings back the point Postman is making : lecturers find it impossible to follow John Cleese's act.

When Postman describes teaching as an amusing activity, and parents comment that "T.V. is so educational", the programme *Sesame Street* usually comes up.

*Sesame Street* offers a well-researched case example for studying the educational effects of television. It was created by child psychologists, teachers and producers to prepare pre-school children for school through pushing basic literacy, numeracy and verbal skills in the programmes. One hope was that the programme would help improve the verbal skills of children deprived of the opportunities for conversation that middle-class children are supposed to have.

However, the gap has not been bridged. Disadvantaged children who watch *Sesame Street* regularly have not made up the ground, neither have they made real progress of any kind. Schools have not been flooded with children whose language is *Sesame Street* enriched. Whilst there are small advances in recognising numbers and letters, child viewers' verbal abilities demonstrate no long-term gains.

The educational benefits of *Sesame Street* were widely publicised in 1970—71 in the U.S.A. by the Educational Testing Service which showed that pre-schoolers learned much from the programmes. These benefits have also been made widely known in this country.

However, the E.T.S. research was criticised severely by the Russell Sage Foundation in *Sesame Street Revisited*, published in 1975. The report found that the gap between advantaged and disadvantaged children may have *become wider*, as a consequence of watching *Sesame Street*.

Furthermore, the heavy viewers of *Sesame Street* received visits from interested researchers, were given programme-related materials and were stimulated to watch more attentively by parental involvement. In fact, *Sesame Street* Revisited" indicated that the key factor in children's progress was *the adult encourage-*

ment of and interest in the experiment, rather than the programmes. To back this up, light viewers showed more gains in cognitive skills than heavy viewers in the group of 'unencouraged' children in the E.T.S. research.

*Sesame Street' Revisited*, then, shows the minimal, and even negative learning effects of a programme specifically designed to educate. Whilst the Nuffield survey showed that for normal children, aged 10−11 and 13−14, ordinary television viewing does not benefit either way and may even be harmful to those likely to become tele-addicts − the Russell Sage Research shows that a deliberately 'educational' programme hardly educates pre-school children.

*Sesame Street* − is also fast paced, and causes overstimulation in young children. Dr. Werner I Halpern of the Rochester Mental Health Clinic noticed a sudden rise of referrals of two year olds with behavioural problems. There were symptoms of restlessness, hyperactivity, inappropriate speech, compulsive serialising of letters and numbers, lack of ability to play, a preference for things over people. Tests showed the children were not autistic, psychotic etc. − Dr Halpern found that they all watched a lot of television, in particular *Sesame Street*. On ceasing T.V. viewing, the children's symptoms vanished and their behaviour became normal. [26]

Postman uses *Sesame Street* to make several points. The fact that parents used T.V.as a babysitter would be offset by its 'educational impact'. It relieves parents of the task of reading with pre-school children. It is entertaining and teaches children to love school, "only if school is like Sesame Street". It represents a style of learning hostile to learning in a school environment. Above all, says Postman, it teaches children to love television. Twenty years on from the first programmes in 1969, *Sesame Street* is still being shown in the U.K. on Channel 4.

## Summary : passive attitudes to learning.

There are many points to summarise. Television is undermining literacy, the acquisition of language at an early age, has displaced reading, rigidifies the imagination, limits play, influences sleeping and dream life adversely, distorts children's sense of reality, teaches consumerism, overstimulates, is often used as a babysitter in institutional as well as family settings, and is a thief of children's time.

While television may be valuable in supplying information on specific educational programmes used in limited ways, the attitudes of passivity, of 'entertain me' encouraged by the medium, are dangerous to the essence of education.

One of the basic aims of education is to encourage attitudes of active responsibility of pupils for their learning and development, as a preparation for them as adults to care for their self-education throughout life.

In conclusion, two primary teachers wrote that the educational effects of television were, 'all the more evident when one comes across the rare child who has no television. These children seem better motivated, more imaginative and generally more mature than their (viewing) peers'.

# Chapter Eight

## *Television and social development: school for violence?*

### *Turning off the process of becoming human?*

There remains the question of the effects of television on children's social development. Television has become a "third parent", hence the title of this book *Who's Bringing Them Up?* Television has had a huge impact on children's lives, such that Neil Postman has observed "the disappearance of childhood" and Marie Winn has written about "children without childhood". Several generations have grown up from birth with T.V. as a "third parent".

Psychologist Urie Bronfenbrenner observed how the socialisation of children within the family can be turned off by viewing:—

> The major impact of television is *not the behaviour it produces, but the behaviour it prevents.* When the television set is on, it freezes everybody; they're all expressionless, focused on the image on the screen, and everything that used to go on between people — the games, the arguments, emotional scenes, out of which personality and ability develop — is stopped. So when you turn on television, you turn off the process of making human beings human.[1]

The aim of this chapter is to explore the effects of television on family life, on anti-social behaviour, on moral development, on relationships and on childhood itself. So far, the book has been mainly concerned with the effects of excessive T.V. watching, regardless of content. This chapter will be more concerned with the effects of programme content.

### '*Without a Television we would not be a Family*'

This was said by a ten year old to his teacher. For many families, viewing is the major activity. Bits of conversation, eating, homework, even reading are carried out in front of the television. Most living rooms are nowadays not focused on the fireplace as formerly, but are arranged for the most convenient viewing. Television dominates the social life of many families – and now increasingly there are sets in each room so that different programmes may be watched by separate members of the family.

Many younger parents, having themselves been brought up with television, cannot imagine a family and social life without its all-pervasive influence. It is the rare family which has experienced both a television dominated social life, and a life without television.

A mother of seven children wrote in an account of her television influenced life in an isolated Lancashire farmhouse. She found television a welcome relief on dark evenings, although she never allowed her babies to watch.

She recalls local mothers telling her they put their babies to sleep beneath the set as it 'seemed to make them sleep better'.*

However, the family moved to a village in Argyll, where television reception is very poor – as a result of which her two youngest, a baby and a toddler have never watched. She observed that: 'It could, of course, be coincidence that Jean (the toddler) is a naturally bright and very talkative child; but is it such a coincidence that she is extremely descriptive and colourful in her talking and seems to have much stronger 'character' than the other at the same age. Since moving her other children,'...have all improved in the social field. The community spirit here, in this small village, is extremely strong, the contrast between life in this village and the one in Lancashire that we left is amazing – young help old and vice versa – projects arise, one after the other and in winter there is so much activity here that one has trouble keeping up the the pace! I'm convinced that this is a natural state of society without television'.

The fundamental question here is how families cultivate their social and cultural life as unique groups with particular identities. In a

---

* (Health visitors, doctors and midwives confirm this practice as very widespread. For example one Stroud doctor, on turning off a T.V. set which was on immediately in front of a new born baby, was told by the parent that the midwife had recommended this as a way of putting restless babies to sleep. In fact local health visitors actively discourage this practice as very unhealthy for the baby).

family where the children watch television for twenty to thirty hours weekly, and the adults watch for the national average of seventeen hours, television will tend to crowd out everything else. Sports, gardening, games, songs, story-telling, conversation, regular meal times, outings, hobbies, homework, visiting with friends and relatives – all the fabric of activities that constitutes a family's 'social culture' will be crowded out. Such a heavy or 'average' viewing television family may therefore suffer from 'cultural poverty'. This condition is no respecter of economic backgrounds – I know poor families with no television (or where it is strictly limited), with rich, varied cultural lives, and I know families which are well-off with a poor family culture.

A major effect of television on the social culture of families is the disruption of the daily, weekly, monthly and yearly rhythms. Each family has its own pattern of getting up, breakfasting, parent(s) getting off to work, children leaving for school, lunchtime, coming back home, suppertime, evening activities and bedtime. The pattern may vary according to the day of the week, the season of the year or holidays. There is a continuum of families on the one hand which are quite irregular about their daily rounds, and on the other, those families which are stuck in a fixed routine. In the middle are families which are neither haphazard nor strict in their daily rituals, but which have worked out a basic rhythm for the day which may be varied according to need.

For children, a rhythmic pattern to the day is an essential element in cultivating stability, a factor that can produce decisiveness and other qualities such as responsibility. A deeper wisdom working in the child seems to sense this and expresses itself in the basic conservatism of children. Regular mealtimes, bedtimes, story times and naps after lunch, give them a secure framework in which to grow.

Television has gradually encroached on the daily life rhythms of families. First, it took over the evening, then bedtime and after school time, followed by lunch time and breakfast time as well.

One mother described how television gradually took over her family. They bought their first set in 1964, the year of their second child's birth. When the children were at primary school, viewing was only allowed for such programmes as *Blue Peter*, and they switched off at 6 p.m. to allow for bedtime stories. The mother was then a teacher for six years and had much less time for family viewing. After leaving her job she fell into the habit of watching more, especially with her husband who had relaxed into watching television all evening. As the children became teenagers, they wanted to watch more, partly under the pressure of friends who watched late night programmes, and pressure from school to watch certain films for educational purposes. From limited family viewing, a daily marathon evolved, not to mention weekends or holidays. Homework was rushed for television's sake, and exam courses neglected.

It is easy to sympathise with such a situation, for like the baby cuckoo brought up by the unsuspecting 'host' parents, television tends to crowd out other family activities. Unless parents are strict, consistent and patient, it is relatively easy for limited viewing to turn into television marathons.

One could argue that there is 'nothing wrong with television', particularly is Britain where *to date*, there has been about fifteen hours' children's programmes per week. The problem of excessive viewing, or the lack of creative activities in the home, is mainly one of parenting skills and control. Parenting is a complex job — switching on the T.V., however, is easy.

A major advantage of television for parents is that it is such an effective drug. It is an instant baby sitter, an electronic child-minder. It shuts children up, stops them demanding things and quarrelling. For hard-pressed mothers after school — in 'rush hour' as we call it in our family — when the evening meal is being prepared it can be a god-send. But it is not only an effective baby sitter and child-minder, it is also used as a sedative in such institutional settings as hospitals, and in my experience, even by a few school teachers. For example, Bel Mooney described her two day visit to Great Ormond Street Children's Hospital in London. She noted the numbers of television trolleys, and how many children were watching. The small playroom in one ward was full of books and toys, but dominated by a large colour T.V. which was on most of the time. She noted that in 1983 a charity had spent £566.00 on treats and outings, £3,235.00 on books and toys, £5,995.00 on play-leaders — and £7,382 on T.V.'s and aerial sockets.[2]

However, since television producers and some educationalists have so easily convinced the majority of people that television is 'educational', parents too are now often convinced it is an 'educational' child-minder.

Television is used in high viewing families as a way to avoid too much inter-personal contact, and is a means by which conversation or working out problems may be prevented. Indeed, the art of conversation has suffered under the impact of television — such conversation as there is, being about television topics. Visitors may arrive to be greeted, to talk a little and then settle in to viewing — for few people seem able to turn off the set. Many wives who have been busy and alone with the children see their husbands come home only to park themselves in front of the television. A 1980 study by the Roper Organisation found that 4,000 men and women claimed that money was the commonest cause of marital conflict, television and children were second — producing three times more arguments than sex.

Whilst families are viewing, they are not engaged in communal activities that may build up their lives together. Viewing could be considered as an anaesthetic that undermines the family. High viewing also prevents children being played with, conversed with, read to or being paid the necessary attention.

Bringing up young children without television can be a challenge. Parents have to keep a look out for potential accidents with toddlers, to stimulate a new play activity when the old one flags, nappies need changing, the repairman comes whilst a fight is starting, a story needs to be read — and so it goes on.

Every family is different. Our "survival aids" as parents are traditional ones. When all the children were young, (two, four and six), they got up early and played happily — especially if there was a small snack or "surprise". Children keep going well if not hungry! This gave us an extra half hour in bed. They normally played happily — individually or together for most of the morning. Play areas, an art and craft table, a nature table, play house, the regular story, kept them going. Nap or quiet time, enabled us to do the housework, work, or snatch a sit down. At "Rush-hour" — from five to six-thirty, when either my wife or myself came home from work, one relieved the situation with a game or story whilst the other made supper. The children were usually in bed by seven at the latest in winter. There was always a bedtime story, "the story of the day's events", a song or two and a prayer.

Now the children are older, the pattern has changed — with a sixteen, a thirteen, and an eleven year old busy with sport, homework, music, arts, crafts, reading — or playing with our six year old. Things are easier after the "young family" stage. Our youngest hardly ever watches, the older choose one or two programmes per week if they remember to.

We have noticed with friends the 'vicious viewing circle' at work.

Toddlers exposed to television seem less able to play, to occupy themselves creatively, to get on with other children — consequently, they may become 'difficult' and the only way out is more viewing which makes things worse. Heavy viewing may cause sleep disturbances, so nap times disappear, 'quiet times' are disrupted by children wanting to watch television, and instead of the state of 'I'm bored Mummy!' being a challenge for mother and child to find a new activity, there is always television.

So television is the perfect answer to demanding children and to the 'nothing to do' syndrome. But as viewing has taken over the traditional role of socialising children, many families consider they would not be families without a television.

Not only has television affected family life fundamentally, it has been a cause in the decline of participation in public life. People watch *Coronation Street* instead of drinking in their local pub. Sports are watched instead of people actually playing them. People watch the election instead of going to local meetings or debates. I remember when television 'hit' a village known to me well in the early 1960s. For several years, the pub-talk was crippled by the box, whist drives became annual rather than monthly, church attendance decreased and societies flagged. Fortunately, in this case, the 'disease' ran its course, and social life recovered.

Many commentators maintain that television has created a more informed public; however, people who watch television an average amount may be less informed than light or non—viewers. Surveys show that very few people even remember one item of television news. One survey, for example, in which viewers were interviewed straight after a news bulletin, showed that more than half could not remember a single item. [3]

Heavy viewing has produced 'private citizens' who are largely dissociated from community life, and who may be socially isolated, even in families. Martin Pawley pictures this world as *The Private Future* in which television is the glue that holds our consumer society together, whilst its citizens are isolated and their perception of social reality fragmented.

Instead of people 'constructing' social reality themselves through conversation over the garden fence, in the shops, on the corner, outside school, in the factory or in the home, television produces its own version of social reality. Pawley writes that: —

Television, queen of the consumer durables, is also the principal assassin of public life and community politics. It absorbs the deceptions, and the evasions of the real world, mixes them with its own, fragmentary glimpses of the real thing that occasionally prompt outraged citizens to write to the newspapers. The crisis of television begins when you stop watching it. Until then it exudes secondary reality, the synthetic glue of consumer society.[4]

## Television and anti-social behaviour

Social skills are learnt by children in the process of being with and relating to other children and adults. This interaction is a two-way process. The television experience is a one-way process which is inherently unsocial − one is relating to an object whilst viewing, rather than a real person. There is no substitute for being with real people in order to learn how to behave in company.

If we recall how children pass through differing stages of consciousness, then we can understand why 'watching' tends to keep the child in an immature relationship to other human beings.

The child before the age of twelve sees the world as pictures of objects to which he has to make a relationship. Up to six or seven years of age, tables, chairs, cats, dolls are all personified quite naturally by a child unaffected by high technology. After seven years his emotional life becomes engaged but the world of experience is still 'outside' him. It is only after eleven to twelve years, when the first intimations of puberty are projecting into his inner world of feelings that what he sees happening around him is related to himself on a personal level. Describe to a class of eleven year olds the more gory happenings of Roman history, the account of Caesar's murder, for instance, and one can see by the expression on their faces to which of them this is still an 'outer' event and which children are 'living' into Caesar's own feelings and experience in a personal imagination of what is taking place.

Therefore, watching T.V. tends to keep the child in the earlier stage of consciousness, continuing to relate to other people as if they were objects, instead of individuals with feelings, ideas and experiences of their own. Certain 'unfeeling' crimes may have been influenced in this way, for if one is conditioned to relate to people as objects on the screen, this can carry over into 'switching people off' in a cold uninvolved fashion.

Erma Bombeck once wrote:—

> During a single evening I saw twelve people shot, two tortured, one dumped into a swimming pool, two cars explode, a rape, and a man who crawled two blocks with a knife in his stomach. I didn't feel anger or shock or horror or excitement or repugnance. The truth is I didn't feel. Through repeated assaults of one violent act after another, you have taken from me something I valued — something that contributed to my compassion and caring — the instinct to feel.[5]

The converse of treating others like objects to be switched on or off is learning to relate to oneself as an object. Each child acquires a precious 'sense of identity' or self-hood in the process of relating with others. This 'ego' or self is nurtured, built up and developed with and through people. Whilst being absorbed totally into the 'blank state' of viewing, young children's ego development may be stultified.

Highly-prized social skills include the ability to communicate clearly through accurate speaking and attentive listening. Learning such essential communication habits is made difficult by television which is a one-way medium which many viewers watch whilst not really watching and listen to whilst not really attending, often as "background".

Young children acquire such social abilities in interaction with other whilst playing, where there are all kinds of possible arguments, quarrels, tiffs, opportunities for co-operation and solving problems. Playing is essential for children, who thereby learn to be socially creative and acquire the ability to play 'the social game' later on. Hence, the play-deprived child will also be a socially-deprived child.

Being able to respond to situations actively is another social attribute. My six year old daughter, for example, was very quick to pick up our two year old or protect him from possible dangers. Looking after him was a training in presence of mind. However, responsiveness to social situations (responsibility really means the 'ability to respond') is blunted by the spectator attitudes taught by television. An experiment has demonstrated this hypothesis.

A non-viewing group of children, and a group that had watched a television for eight minutes, were asked to watch two younger children and fetch adult help if anything happened. The viewing group took significantly longer to react than the non-viewers, and more of them failed to respond. Simply put, viewing trains children not to respond. Perhaps this is a reason why in so many emergencies or situations where presence of mind is required, some people react like spectators, 'as if it was on T.V.'

Another social effect of the television *medium* is the tetchiness, touchiness, or even aggressiveness, observed in many children after viewing. According to the Emerys, such behaviour may not result from the *content* of a programme, but may be caused by the *act of viewing* itself. They put forward the hypothesis that, '...the old brain, that part which we share more closely with other mammals and lower order species, and that part which is tied more directly to emotional concerns, will be released from direct control of the higher centre during viewing with some quite predictable consequences for the viewer...' They continue, 'Impulsivity and aggression after viewing, long expected to be a result of programmed violence, may well turn out to be an inevitable result of *viewing per se*'.[6]

Hyperactive behaviour in children may be caused partly by viewing. The continual changing of visual frames and the attention-getting technical tricks force a short attention-span in children. The inbuilt needs for playful activities which are dammed up by passive viewing may result in children bursting out into activity afterwards. The fast, forced electronic pace of the screen images, which are produced far more rapidly than our brain can consciously take in, may 'speed up' children with a hyperactive predisposition. The Emerys, in linking the rapid increase in hyperactive children to viewing on similar grounds to those mentioned above, believe that there were good reasons for predicting that as colour television becomes widespread in Australia, the incidence of hyperactivity will come closer to the higher American level. [7]

Parents always ask whether television viewing encourages anti-social behaviour and violent responses in children. There is a vast amount of research for and against T.V. as a school for violence" − the "experts" have been arguing for years about this. Since researchers are not agreed, it is important for parents to make their own observations and judgements. So is viewing a school for violence?

## *Viewing — a school for violence?*

Initially, I was reluctant to write about the effects of content on viewers, which I believed was up to individuals to make up their minds about. I still think that the effects of the television medium itself — just watching — may be far more influential on anti-social behaviour than the effects of programmed violence. But so much sound research has linked programmed violence to the rise in violence in society, and so many people in my T.V. talks are concerned about this, that the question of viewing 'as a school for violence' needs to be faced.

The more sensational aspects of television violence need to be scrutinised carefully. Perhaps it is the already disturbed children who imitate violence seen on the television, like the boy who hanged himself after seeing a similar incident on a western, or the American girl who was raped with a bottle soon after such an act was televised. It is well known that in Ulster the para—militaries plan their acts of violence to gain maximum news coverage, and that 'highlighted' violence such as the *one* scuffle on an otherwise peaceful day's picketing, is 'good' television. The news media often seem to have an inherent need for such highlights — I remember in February 1980 one commentator saying of a large secondary picket at Sheerness Steel Works, 'Unfortunately, the day has been something of an anti-climax...' A story is not newsworthy unless there is a conflict.

However, such sensational effects may not be so significant as the gradual changes in ideas, attitudes, values and behaviour that constant viewing may produce in children. George Gerbner's work at the Annenberg School of Communications on how television moulds people's view of the social world underlines this point. Heavy viewers not only overestimate the likelihood of encountering violence, exaggerate potential dangers, have a leaner and meaner view of the world, are more fearful and distrustful than light viewers — they are also more likely to invest in security devices such as burglar alarms and large dogs. Perception leads to behaviour. Television programmes tend to produce a climate of expected violence, according to Gerbner. Expected violence can lead to self fulfilling prophecies. The I.B.A. researcher, Dr Mallory Wober, considers this finding of Gerbner's work one of the most serious challenges to television.

People linking televised violence to increasing social violence use figures like the Home Office's, which shows that "violence" has

multiplied ten times since 1951, when T.V.use began to spread in
Britain. They point to the fact that children who watch an average of
three hours a day, over a thousand hours a year, may see thousands of
violent incidents by the time they are sixteen. With the unmonitored
use of home videos, the situation could be much worse. Even though
in Britain, the BBC "count" for violent incidents is an average of two
per hour, it might be better for readers to carry out their own survey.
One parent who did such a survey on "harmless" children's programmes, because his daughter was suffering from T.V. induced
nightmares, was so shocked by the nature of the screened incidents,
that he got rid of the set altogether. The UK "watershed" is 9 p.m.,
after which the more violent programmes are watched. However
many children watch after nine and a large proportion of parents do
not exercise control over what is being watched.

Researchers Jerome and Dorothy Singer of Yale University are
concerned about the hazards for children growing up in a television
environment. They put forward the point that the television industry
calls for proof that viewing produces negative side-effects in children:

> Thus we have the intriguing paradox of a tremendously success-
> ful industry that earns its income through the sale of advertising
> time, using claims that a company's influence, brand recognition,
> and sale of products are enhanced through regular viewing of
> these commercials – yet at the same time, industry represent-
> atives assert that heavy viewing by children of a variety of
> frightening or anti-social behaviours on the same medium will
> not influence their behaviour! Each new study by social scientists
> that suggests that viewing aggressive materials may indeed have
> some influence on the overt behaviour of children or on their
> attitudes is greeted by an extremely critical analysis...

The Singers, in reviewing their own research and that of many other
social scientists, concluded that:

> ...heavy television viewing puts children at risk of increased
> aggression and restlessness with all the negative cognitive and
> social consequences of such a behaviour pattern (Friedrich –
> Lofer and Huston, 1986; Huesman and Eron, 1984; Singer
> 1984). Those of us who have been active over more than 15 years
> in studying a variety of aspects of the television medium in a

reasonably scientific fashion cannot fail to be impressed with the significance of this medium for the emerging consciousness of the developing child. In its present form, both from the stand-point of content and of its fast paced, fragmented format (Singer 1980), we can only conclude that the frequent unmonitored television viewing by young children puts them at risk...

With the competition of a television set in the home attracting their growing children, parents are going to have to decide early on whose values they want to develop, the parents' or the television's world of violence."[9]

## *Notel, Unitel, and Multitel : a naturalistic experiment.*

The Singers refer to Tannis Williams' study of how television came to "Notel", a town previously without television, and its effects on children.

Tannis Williams found that the aggressive behaviour of Notel children "increased significantly following the introduction of television". Her conclusions were based on observations of children's behaviour. The effects showed up in both girls and boys, and for verbal and physical aggression. Children initially low in aggression showed increases, not just the children initially high in aggression. These effects were so marked as to be observed two years after television came to Notel. The results could not be explained by IQ differences or to social class. T.V. viewing in general, rather than specific programmes, seemed to be the cause.[10]

How, then, does television viewing affect the behaviour of children? What are the mechanisms and processes?

### *Imitation*

Young children learn through imitation, through copying other people. The "role models" they experience are important for their development and social learning. So the imitation of aggressive models through vicarious learning could increase children's verbal and physical aggression. Sporadic attention to violent highlights, the lack of under-standing by young children of the links between aggressive actions and punishments which are portrayed, may be mechanisms. Scenes of aggressive interaction, when shown many times, and which are seldom counteracted, could be copied by children.

So just as children may learn positive social behaviour from television – such as a child saving the life of another child from suffocation by dislodging a bone, having seen the method demonstrated on television – so behaviour can be learned from negative role models.

That children imitate toughs was proved by W.A.Belson in an exhaustively scientific study of a sample of 1565 London boys in 1972–73, who were interviewed about their viewing habits and attitudes to violence. Dr. Belson found that, even taking into account over 227 variables such as size, physical strength, family size, neighbourhood or divorce in the family, television violence had an effect external to these factors. One conclusion was, 'The evidence is strongly supportive of the hypothesis that long-term exposure to television violence increases the degree to which boys engage in serious violence'.[11]

## Immunisation, desensitisation and disinhibition.

As well as the imitation of and identification with aggressive role models, T.V. violence may immunise and desensitise children. By violence, I mean physical or mental injury, hurt or death inflicted on people or animals. By viewing violence regularly, one can become immunised against violence and horror. As a result it may be accepted as a natural part of life. Children exposed to violence on television were found to have less emotional arousal to violence.

*Desensitization* is a process which whittles away normal feelings in people, until they can be relaxed and at ease whilst watching events that would have otherwise aroused the gravest concern. The thousands of killings, the murders, fights and other violent incidents shown on television may be aptly described as mass desensitization.

Another factor is that *television removes inhibitions* in people which would otherwise prevent them from behaving violently. Through disinhibition, people feel no longer hampered by feelings of guilt, shame or embarrassment. One experiment was set up to demonstrate the disinhibiting effect of a violent film. Subjects were asked to administer 'electric shocks' to another person when they made a mistake. In fact, the victim only pretended to suffer. Of two groups, the members of the first who had seen a knife fight from 'Rebel

Without a Cause' punished mistakes more severely than those in the second group who had only seen a harmless education film.

Violent methods of solving problems and conflicts in everyday life situations are frequently shown on television, and this may cause disinhibition.

## Stereotyping.

Another form of violence is the portrayal of groups of people in stereotyped ways — for example gender role stereotyping, ageism, and racism. Stereotyping does violence to people because the process undermines the ability to see and relate to people as individuals.

In Notel, Williams found that children's "...sex-role attitudes, that is, beliefs about appropriate and typical behaviour for girls and boys, were more strongly sex-typed in the presence than in the absence of television."[12]

One rarely sees older female presenters on television. A study of advertising showed that men tended to be portrayed as providers, rational, independent — whilst the women were portrayed as dependent, home bound, and gave emotional reasons for buying products.

There can be considerable bias in reporting about groups of people. For example one news content analysis found that conflict events such as arms finds, shootings, bombings, accounted for 20% of news stories in British or Irish newspapers. However, these stories accounted for 50% of news items on Irish or British T.V. There was a complete lack of reporting on other Northern Irish news, such as strikes, beauty queens and employment questions.[13]

To conclude, the processes of stereotyping, observational learning, imitation, identification, immunisation, desensitization, physical arousal, disinhibition and justification (i.e. the violence of T.V. heroes justifies the aggression of viewers) may be causes of increased anti-social behaviour.

## Moral development and the uninvited guest.

Questions of the influence of television programmes relate to our personal views about the process of children's social and moral development. Whatever our values as adults — whether we are catholics, puritans, humanists, greens — children will take a long time to develop their own values.

Young children imitate and absorb the standards of behaviour of those around them, especially their parents. They do as you do, not as you say. They will behave in certain ways because they are expected to, notions of 'right' and 'wrong' are conformed to rather than understood. For example, should a five year old be asked if someone who drops five plates by accident has behaved worse than another who smashed one intentionally, the most likely answer is to be the former person. At this age quantity and size carries a moral implication. Whilst a 'provisional' socially influenced conscience may have developed by the primary school years, it is not until the turning point of the tenth year that children begin to grasp notions of their personal responsibility, to accept codes of behaviour and respond to reasoned arguments about right and wrong. It then takes the teenage years to develop an 'inner conscience' and a more conscious awareness of alternative values.

In this process of moral development from an early age, then, imitation is how a child learns. Aristotle believed that man was 'the most imitative creature in the world and learns by imitation'. In behaviour, 'each seeks to transfer to himself the traits he admires in the other'. Because imitative learning by young children is so central to their development, they soak up models, behaviour and words like sponges. As parents it is possible for us to create a positive environment where children have wholesome models to imitate. For example, my wife is firm with my occasional lapses into bad language in front of our children — although my efforts were rendered useless by grandpa's visit, after which Daniel delighted in calling people 'lucky devils!'

Young children, for whom 'seeing is believing', see many desirable and undesirable models of behaviour on television. Unfortunately, in spite of attempts to make a programme's content 'pro-social', it is difficult to portray subtle emotions like respect, care and love, or complex moral situations where 'there but for fortune, go you or I'. It is easier to programme high-lighted incidents, such as anger, physical, or violent incidents, because these come across 'better' on the low definition television screen.

One study by Gomberg illustrates the reactions of some New York four year olds to television content. They said such things as, 'All people on television were either all good or all bad... All cowboys were good people whereas all Indians were bad... All men in the army were good'. Less widely held views were, 'Bad people bleed but good people don't... A bad man never does anything that is good... The job of the cowboy is to kill the Indian'.

A four year old was found in the playground, profoundly upset because he had grazed his knee. He was shouting 'I am not bad, not bad'. Apparently in his mind only the bad people bleed.

The children also had views on violence such as: —

'All the good people had to kill the bad people'. 'A gun means you are strong'. 'All the quarrels between good and bad end in killing'.

Such ideas were applied to everyday life: 'If bad people try to kill you, call our mother and she will get a gun and kill him; every good person loves little children'. [14]

Such examples from America, where televised violence is much greater than here, are perhaps extreme ones. Certainly in British television programmes aimed at young children, great care is taken to show 'prosocial' programmes. But just speaking as a parent, I would prefer not to have to explain the kinds of unusual behaviour my own young children occasionally see on adult programmes. One mother told of how disturbed her twelve year old daughter was at seeing a difficult, harrowing childbirth. They were unable to switch off the set in time, and the episode came on without warning.

Television may provide unexpected models for imitation which are impossible to control, unless one has detailed fore-knowledge of a programme. Hence, television can become the 'uninvited guest' in the home, providing all kinds of models for one's children to imitate. This guest may use poor language, may be violent, aggressive, and rude, and do things not normally seen or permitted in the family. Not only *what* this guest does will be imitated but *how* he affects behaviour may have even worse consequences such as increasing hyperactivity.

Whether — and to what extent   parents wish the 'uninvited guest' to influence their children is up to each individual's choice.

## *Children without childhood:* — *the disappearing child and the hurried child*

One conclusion drawn by writers such as Marie Winn and Neil Postman is that television is a major force undermining childhood, which was once understood as a long, sheltered period in which children were gradually introduced into the adult world.

Marie Winn describes children growing up too fast, who become sophisticated, mini-adults before they are out of grade school. Infancy and childhood have been merged into a intense bout of three to five years of parenting, plus some extra years of loosening apron strings. By ten, they are apparently knowledgeable and sophisticated, innocence has been replaced by cynicism and "teenage" activities are common for "weeny−boppers"!. Whilst she discusses the divorce rate, both parents working (the "child care gap"), the break up of traditional family patterns, the lack of structure, as causes − she also mentions the widespread belief that, "children are adults' psychological and emotional equals and as such deserve autonomy and independence." She believes that the marketing of "adult children" on television, and the replacement by "television's moronic and crass world" of children's play, reading, family activities and conversation − have also been major causes.[15]

The "disappearing child" was observed by Neil Postman in his *Age of Show Business*[16] Noting that television consists mainly of "stories and pictures" he asks:−

> What is the effect on grown-ups of a culture dominated by pictures and stories? What is the effect of a medium that is entirely centred on the present; that has no capability of revealing the continuity of time? What's the effect of a medium that must abjure conceptual complexity and highlight personality? What's the effect of a medium that always asks for an immediate, emotional response?

Postman argues that the television age, which reveals the adult world, has homogenized the 'child' and 'adult' worlds which developed in the print age. T.V. is aimed at the average twelve year old, and requires, no literary skills, to watch. He argues that "child-adults" are depicted by the media, rather than the sort of busy, traditional children one still sees on the British programme, *Blue Peter*. Children's clothing and fashion styles are becoming adult-like. Adult competition is mirrored in the sporting arena, for example: tennis, swimming or baseball. Figures on alcoholism, drug abuse and crime, indicate a fading distinction between childhood and adulthood.

His advice to parents is to limit the amount of T.V. viewing, to

monitor carefully what children are watching and to discuss programmes together. He describes: –

> Such parents are not only helping their children to *have* a
> childhood but are, at the same time, creating a sort of intellectual
> elite. Certainly in the short run the children who grow up in
> such homes, will, as adults, be much favoured by business, the
> professions, and the media themselves. What can we say in the
> long run? Only this: Those parents who resist the spirit of the age
> will contribute to what might be called the Monastery Effect, for
> they will help to keep alive a humane tradition. It is not conceiv-
> able that our culture will forget that it needs children. But it is
> halfway toward forgetting that children need childhood. Those
> who insist on remembering shall perform a noble service.[17]

A more considered argument comes from David Elkind, a developmental psychologist who wrote *The Hurried Child – Growing up too
fast too soon*.[18] He describes hurried children: –

> Hurried children are forced to take on the physical, psychological,
> and social trappings of adulthood before they are prepared to
> deal with them. We dress our children in miniature adult
> costumes, (often with designer labels), we expose them to
> gratuitous sex and violence, and we expect them to cope with an
> increasingly bewildering social environment – divorce, single
> parenthood, homosexuality. Through all these pressure, the
> child senses that it is important for him or her to cope without
> admitting the confusion and pain that accompany such changes.
> Like adults, they are made to feel they must be survivors, and
> surviving means adjusting – even if the survivor is only four or
> six or eight years old.

By hurrying children, we put them under great stress – 'teach Johnny
to read at four', accelerate learning, computing at five. "Readiness"
and developmental phases are forgotten as children are viewed as
miniature adults. Elkind describes many of the means of hurrying
children – and includes television, with its vast extension of the
human senses, the exposure to children of the adult world, the fast
paced stress of programmes, the commercial push and the sorts of
precocious children portrayed. Television may cause information and

emotional overloads — children know much more than they can understand. Too much information is given too quickly, according to Elkind, and children may not be emotionally or intellectually ready for this information.

# PART II

*How to break the television habit.*

# Chapter Nine

## *How to break the television habit.*

There are several reasons why it is important to break the T.V. habit, or to prevent the habit arising in the first place. Young children need to live their own lives, discovering themselves through play, family activities and conversation — protected from the overwhelming stimulation of both the T.V. medium and the programme content. For this reason, an influential educationalist called Dorothy Cohen observed that: —

> The impact of television on so-called disadvantaged children has been minimal in terms of goals such as learning to read — but its impact on their development had been great. It has robbed them of their normal opportunities to talk, to play, to *do*. It has interfered with their normal opportunities to grow. The big thing for me is the protection of children during the period of vulnerability in their lives. I think children under five should not watch television at all.

There are other reasons — we want our children to become *themselves*, not heavily packaged by T.V.. T.V., according to Neil Postman and Marie Winn, is eroding 'childhood' itself. Children need protection and gradual introduction to the world. Children do not need 'entertaining' all the time. "Boredom" is often the transition to engaging in another play activity.

## *Watching too much television?*

You may want to ask some questions about children to see if they watch too much television:

1. Do they watch breakfast television before school?
2. Do they get up with the set on in their bedrooms?
3. Is Saturday morning T.V. watched?
4. Do they watch T.V. straight after school?
5. Are they often bored?
6. Does the family watch during meals? How much conversation is T.V.related?

7.  Is the television on as background to children playing with their friends and toys?
8.  Is television the most time consuming activity?
9.  Do they do homework with the set on?
10. Do they want family life geared to whats on television?
11. Can they occupy themselves for sustained periods of time?
12. Do they want junk food and T.V. advertised toys?

Some other questions posed by Joan Wilkins in her *Breaking the T.V. Habit* may also help identify children who watch too much: —

1.  Does your child want instant gratification? Does she lack tolerance — always wanting quick solutions to problems?
2.  Are there "behaviour problems" such as anti-social, aggressive play, restlessness, poor self control and hyperactivity?
3.  Is your child overtired and listless?
4.  Are there tasks and responsibilites which are avoided? Is there a problem of relating to people?
5.  Does your child have many fears and nightmares which may be T.V. related?
6.  How much "T.V.talk" is there? How good is the child at speaking?
7.  Is there a problem with schoolwork?
8.  Can the child turn the set off at the end of a programme?

Such questions may help you judge the extent to which a child is a 'telly addict'. Having read this book, you may have considered how television affects children and family life. You may have been convinced already that *you* were a tele—addict, but needed a practical path to controlling your viewing! Of course, you may also be quite satisfied with your family's viewing habits.

Often, a "crisis" such as the set breaking down, a steep rise in the licence fee, financial hardship, a long television—less period such as a summer holiday, a particular incident where your child is upset by T.V. — may spark — off a re-appraisal of television. Joan Wilkins recommends a four week programme to overcome the T.V. habit. The first step is to monitor for a week just how much the family and its members watch.

## 1.  *Monitoring viewing for a week*

Some families keep a daily record of their viewing — who is watching, what programmes, when and for how long? Parents can check whether they are using television as a babysitter. Who watches alone? Are sets on with no one in particular watching? Are sets on whilst there are visitors?

The results can be interesting. Most families are amazed at how much the television is on — and children may find that their parents, especially Dad, may be heavier viewers than they are.

Whilst watching together, one can begin to become critical viewers. How many commercials are there? What technical methods are used to maintain viewer's attention? Observe each other watching — analyse and discuss the content of programmes.

Most people are very surprised at how much they watch. This discovery leads to Wilkins' next step, which is to take a critical look at what you watch.

## 2.  *Taking a critical look.*

Keep watching yourself and your family watching, but view more critically. At the beginning of the week, look together at the T.V. Times and discuss which programmes you would like to watch and why. Again, each day review which programmes you and your children are going to watch. Keep a record of how good the programme was in terms of interest, quality, appropriateness for children's viewing, entertainment, information, language etc. With discussion, one may find many programmes are not worth watching — and that other activities may become more attractive.

## 3.  *Cutting back.*

During the third week, try applying some of Joan Wilkins' guidelines as ways of cutting back on viewing: —

1.  Put away all T.V. sets except one — and cover this with a cloth. 'Out of sight, out of mind.'

2.  Stop viewing before school and during meals.
3.  Decide on three school nights and afternoons when the T.V. is off.
4.  Allow only one hour (or 1 programme) on each of the remaining school nights.
5.  Decide as a family about the number of viewing hours at weekends.
6.  On Sunday, choose which programmes you will watch as a family, and as individuals, during the following week.

There are "good T.V. viewing habits" to encourage, such as encouraging active viewing by discussing and preparing for a programme beforehand; sit at least ten feet away from the set; try watching for techniques, character portrayals and motivations to remain "awake"; watch a programme with your children and discuss it afterwards, there may be follow up activities such as books, conversation and making things.

## 4.  *Life without television*

Try turning off the television for a week and keeping it off, that is, if you feel that there are many other things to do.

Put the remaining T.V. set in a cupboard or store-room. Avoid the *T.V.Times* by not buying it, and remove the programme page from the newspaper. Do interesting and enjoyable things at the times of your favourite programmes. Get your children to invite their friends over to play more, read together, take up a hobby or sport. Enjoy the relaxed time!

If you have prepared the way, you will soon find the children won't miss the T.V. if there are other things to do. This is why viewing goes right down in summer. Since children are naturally good at playing, they will soon find things to do with a little parental help. Fill up the vacant spots left by the T.V. sets with some of these suggestions:—

A *play space* — a play area with dress up clothes, dolls house, barn, Wendy house, a special place where children can play such as a play corner.
A *nature table* — for young children to re-create the season, with flowers, fruits, treasures, moss, plants, candles.
A *sports area* — a box, cupboard, with balls, bats, ropes, skipping ropes, skates, rackets — for ballgames, hopscotch, games etc.

*A craft table* – a table where children can paint, draw, make things, sew, knit, make models. There are crayons, paper, card, wool, glue, cloth, scissors, pencils, brushes etc. Make presents for birthdays and Christmas.

*A music area* – this may be a piano, or a corner in the livingroom, where there are instruments, music and where one can play singly or with others. Having things like recorders and guitars around encourages children to become interested in playing.

*Garden play things* – make sure there's a good sandpit, swing, climbing frame, Wendy house and a play area if there is garden.

*Books* – a children's book corner, with shelves and reading space. Read bedtime stories.

It may be difficult to find the time to act on these suggestions in a single week – but it is essential to provide alternative activities to viewing.

Other ideas include an indoor games evening, getting the children to cook a meal once a week, going out to play sports regularly, fixing things, walking, taking up a forgotten hobby, having another family over and taking the children to the library.

There are many resource books which can help – such as Rahima Baldwin's, *You are Your Child's First Teacher, Lifeways, The Children's Year,* and *Festivals, Family and Food* (see Resources : Appendix I.)

When the fourth week with no television is over, many families find life so interesting that they either leave the set in the cupboard, or are well able to watch only limited number of programmes. They can control T.V. and are not controlled by it.

## Getting rid of television overnight : the drastic option.

The four week programme suggested by Joan Wilkins may work well for some families. However, many families choose the drastic option – of getting rid of television altogether, at once. This is the most drastic option, but for those who feel unable to impose strict rules on limited viewing, it may be effective. A good way to become enthusiastic about this option is to imagine how stimulating life without television could become. One mother of four (a single parent family) wrote how they gave up television – her attempts to limit viewing to weekends only and her 'constant anti-T.V. nagging' failed. Her two eldest were

doing exams, the fourteen year old was neglecting his music, and she
felt that her five year old was 'young enough to be saved' before he
became 'hooked': —

We have now been 'without' for eight months, and can honestly
say that we don't miss the thing at all. I know far more about
what's going on at their respective schools, because we now all
sit down in the kitchen and chat over a cup of tea at four o'clock;
we have all discovered the library and the joys of reading again.
We go out together to the theatre, and more importantly, the
children happily settle down to their homework in the evenings,
without the feeling that they're missing something on T.V.

A mother of three, having read one of Faith Hall's letters in a
newspaper embarked similarly on a family life without television.
Most important was that both her husband and she discussed the
matter together and came to a joint agreement. Many attempts fail
because each parent has different opinions, enabling the children to
'divide and rule'. This particular mother wrote: —

After much discussion and thought my husband and I decided
to send back our colour T.V. (we still have a black and white
portable which we use if there is a programme of special interest
we wish to see.) We have three children aged nine, three and one
— all boys. The difference in their behaviour I consider remark-
able. They have discovered that there is a garden outside the
backdoor and are in it whenever weather permits. Their play is
so much more imaginative and less violent than when they used
to watch a lot of T.V. My eldest son reads a lot more, and gets
enjoyment from it, and a big plus from my point of view is that
they don't fight and squabble as much. As for my husband and
myself, we get so much more time for decorating, riding,
playing squash and as we are a musical family, more time for
practising. A local police constable described how much more
time he had for his wife and children after getting rid of their set.
Whilst he and his wife never allowed their young children to
watch, he became a tele-addict — so much so, that his wife said
he was 'just like the lodger'. Because of his vulnerability to
viewing they removed the set — with beneficial consequences
for everyone. Fortunately, there was the work of fixing up their

new house and garden to replace the T.V. habit. Both parents commented how much more involved he had become in putting the children to bed and story telling, for which there had been no time before. One interesting comment by the policeman, who was quite used to coping with tough behaviour on the beat, was 'Before, television violence never bothered me, but now I watch so little, it is hard for me to stand'.

In experiments with families foregoing television for a month, there were similar experiences to those of the two families described above. There was more socializing, conversation, outings and visiting. Meal time became less frenetic. People took up hobbies, sports and read more. Generally, life became more interesting after the initial break. The following family story by Sue Elworthy of Leamington Spa is included because it shows some of the challenges, questions and problems of life without television: —

When we first bought furniture for a flat we did not consider a T.V. necessary. I don't think we even considered getting one. When we bought a house and furniture we didn't think of getting a set. After our children were born the decision not to have a set became more conscious as we observed other children's watching habits. I was distressed to see children sitting hunched up in front of a box instead of playing and thought that no matter how splendid the content was, the passivity of the children was to be avoided. I didn't mind them making the social effort to go to visit a friend to watch a programme. Our eldest boy, when he was eight, had a regular date with a neighbour, who was eighty, on a Thursday evening to watch a programme of archaeology — a subject of mutual interest — and we felt that this was a very pleasant social occasion for him; especially as they exchanged archaeological books and had talks about what they had watched. What we wanted to avoid was the children switching on when at a loose end and regulating their lives around the T.V. programmes.

There is no doubt that life is more demanding without a set. I remember a Friday afternoon when I had a house full of tired children. If there had been a T.V. I would have sat them in front of it, but I didn't have one, so I organised a game of hares and hounds and they ran around the streets chasing each other happily for a couple of hours. I often feel our children and their non-T.V. friends are more noisy and more of a nuisance in the neighbourhood than their T.V. watching counterparts.

Our children enjoy playing with other children very much and are distressed when they visit friends and the T.V. is switched on. Apparently they don't find the programmes very interesting and sometimes feel embarrassment at leaving to find someone who will play with them. The emphasis on play is theirs. To them acceptable play is not role-playing T.V. characters and they will be disparaging about children who play like this.

I have noticed that when children have been watching T.V. for more than an hour they are extremely irritable afterwards. I've noticed this with our own children and non-T.V. neighbours' children but can't say that the T.V. watching variety seems to be affected the same way.

We belong more and more to a minority sub-culture. Our town has a carnival and float after float goes by — all with T.V. connections — and we don't know what it is about. I think this is rather sad. They don't understand the basis of many playground games. We often don't get the jokes in the Pantomine. Sometimes I certainly have doubts about whether we are right in opting out of so much of the culture.

How do we compensate for this deprivation? We read to them much more than we would if we had T.V. They have time to be bored. I think this is very important. Boredom is the seedbed for interests of your own. To deprive a child of the chance to be bored and then respond to the vacuum on his own and become his own person seems a terrible theft. The greatest plus so far has been that they don't seem to mind being different from other children. They probably wouldn't feel so confident about our family's eccentricity if we did not have neighbours who don't watch either.

Another family who gave up overnight were the Allens' from Brighton. The Waldorf or Steiner school they were to send their children to, advises parents that watching television is not healthy for children's development and undermines a creative education. Linda Allen writes about her family's experiences in an article, *Taking away the Television*:

The sound of squabbling in the next room interrupted our discussion on how much television, if any, the children should be watching. We felt it would present problems trying to limit the amount of viewing, and in some ways be easier to remove it altogether. When we realised that this particular squabble was over which channel should be on, we decided to do just that.

They were so busy yelling at each other that the television was unplugged and gone from the room before they realised what was happening. Then a fresh argument broke out on whose fault it was that such drastic action had been taken.

Michael was the first to enquire, most politely, when the television was being returned because he had hoped to watch a particular programme that day. Standing at a safe distance we broke the news that it was a permanent removal. He disappeared to his room in a flurry of temper and disparaging remarks about the Steiner school, of which he was not yet even a member, and the adverse effects it was having on his parents. Steven in his usual style, waited a fortnight before mentioning the television and, as it was expected of him, shed a few tears when I confirmed it was 'gone forever'. Ashley spent a lot of time studying the vacated space on the coffee table, and considering various items we could put there in place of the television. Michael determined to prove there was no possibility of life without television, did his best to remain steeped in misery, and I have to hand it to him that he did this extremely well.

Steven thought about what they could do on Sunday mornings when they usually got up to watch programmes for two hours. I volunteered to get up with them and play a game or tell stories. But Steven had a much better idea; he was longing to try out his newly acquired skill of bread making at home, and Sunday at 7 a.m. seemed an ideal moment. Michael saw my pained expression and immediately seconded the motion, so bread-making it was. We all thoroughly enjoyed it and television ceased to be a part of their daily lives.

The lack of television has been particularly good for Michael. It was quite noticeable that after a couple of hours viewing he was very sullen and often quite moody. Once programmes that interested him came to an end he was at a total loss and couldn't think what to do other than play his computer, and too much of that had a similar effect.

I feel now that because of the television he has failed to develop any special interests or hobbies that I am sure he would otherwise have done. Five months without T.V. and he still finds it difficult sometimes to know what to do with his time. He spends more time in the garden or on his bicycle than he used to. He cooks with me, which he seems to enjoy and talks to us in greater depth and more often than he has done for years. In his room he reads and draws and is currently designing his Christmas cards. All in all there is quite an improvement in his general demeanour and he is not so bad tempered in the mornings. Steven and Ashley spend more time playing together and I really don't think they miss television at all. It's so much better to look in the play room and see them building bricks or making a camp, than staring at a television screen. It's a relief, especially with Christmas approaching, that I haven't got to keep saying "We'll see" to Ashley, in response to his request for every toy available and so enticingly portrayed on the screen. And Steven no longer insists I should hold my washing up to the window to check if I'm using the right soap powder!

(P.S. Jeff would like to point out that although removal of the one-eyed monster from the corner of the room, is definitely beneficial to the children, it must be remembered that denying them their visual Valium will cause troubles unless one is prepared to help them fill the gap with other, more fulfilling activity.)

## Limited, discriminating viewing with clear rules.

A third option is to limit children's viewing within a framework of clear, agreed rules such as:—

— No viewing at all during school week, and only 'special' programmes at weekends.
— No viewing at all below a certain age e.g. for pre-schoolers.
— The choice of several special programmes per week.
— A weekly amount of viewing.
— Viewing limited to specifically children's programmes only.
— No viewing while homework is being done, or before it is completed. Viewing by young children only when adults are present. Programmes must be switched off promptly at the end.

– Only occasional viewing of special programmes for children who have not yet acquired the ability to enjoy reading fluently and regularly.

– No viewing at all on schoolnights.

– No viewing before school, or during meals, on schooldays.

– No television in bedroom. Keep one set working, but put it in one of the less comfortable rooms in the house, so that it is not the focus of the sitting room.

– For every half hour of viewing, one hour should be allocated to sport, reading, playing etc. (One father only let his children watch if they rode an exercise bike which generated enough electricity to run the T.V. set!)

– Only watch programmes selected at the start of the day or week.

– Avoid buying T.V. dominated newspapers or periodicals.

These are only suggested guidelines to choose from – it all depends on what your particular family needs.

The drawback of allowing a set amount of viewing each day, such as half an hour, is that this might be too habit-forming. Avoiding regular viewing at a specific time each day may prevent a habit-forming rhythm being set up.

Parents with a natural authority in their families may have no difficulty in imposing such rules, particularly if these are discussed and the reasons underlying them are understood by the older children. However, children can always go and watch next door, and wear down parents' endurance with such arguments as 'my friends view T.V. a lot more – so why can't I?' Rules without reasons, and rules in families without a lively set of alternative activities may be counter-productive in the long run.

One parent in favour of limited viewing for her four children aged seven to ten, whilst refusing to use television as a baby minder, uses it as 'an effective tool both for education and disciplined entertainment'. She continued:

Fortunately, I am reasonably bossy and have had no difficulty in restricting the amount of time my children have spent viewing. I find they now impose their own restrictions through taste and demands of homework and hobbies and I have noticed the onset of discrimination with pleasure. As I watch with them (perforce and from a sense of genuine obligation) I am able to counterbalance any undesirable impressions they might gain. What I object to is undertones of violence under the guise of truth and realism, in a programme I am unable to preview, screened at children's viewing time (between 4−6), an event which occurs too often.

To be successful, the option of limited viewing within clear rules requires parents to educate their children into a more discriminating use of television, to explain the reasons for their views, and to watch with children. For parents to watch by themselves at a time when children are still about will not be setting a good example. Some families ration their children to half an hour or so before six o'clock, and then the set is switched off until after bedtime so as not to interfere with supper, bedtime stories and going to sleep.

Jim Trelease tells how his family developed their own rules for viewing.[3]

When the Treleases first announced to their two children that viewing was to be restricted, they started to cry − and continued on and off for four months. The reason for limited viewing was that their nine year old daughter and five year old son were showing signs of T.V. addiction. The customary 'read aloud' time each night was deteriorating because the children said, 'it took too much time away from the T.V.' Another factor was seeing how some friends had no T.V. on weekdays for their four children − and the advantages.

The Treleases had to withstand peer group pressure from their children's friends, and from other parents. "And what about the National Geographic Specials?" they would say.

After three months, there was enough time for reading aloud, for books, for unhurried homework, for games, for cooking, for model making, letter writing, sports, painting, drawing, household jobs − and,".... best of all − to talk with each other, ask questions and answer questions"... Our children's imaginations were coming back to life again". Their T.V. plan was as follows:−

1   The television is turned off at supper time and not turned on again until the children are in bed, Monday to Thursday.
2   Each child is allowed to watch one school night show a week (subject to parents' approval). Homework, chores, etc must be finished beforehand.

3 Weekend television is limited to any two of the three nights.
The remaining night is reserved for homework and other activities. The children make their selections separately.

The selection encouraged discriminating viewing and their children
became very choosy. They either forgot the option of a special
programme during the week, or chose not to watch.

However, Jim Trelease observed that: —

If you are going to require children to curtail their T.V. viewing,
if you are going to create a three-hour void in their daily lives,
then *you* must make a commitment to fill that void.

## Growing out of the viewing habit

It is difficult to give up habits once they are established and hence the
effectiveness for some of the 'shock' solution of getting rid of the
television altogether. Habits are often deeply ingrained, as I found out
when having converted our small kitchen to increase its size, my wife
was upset with me for months because 'things weren't where they
were supposed to be'.

It is said that when the cavalier William Penn was converted to
Quakerism, he was worried about carrying a sword amongst the
pacifist Friends. He asked George Fox if he should get rid of his
sword, but the great mystic said, 'Wear thy sword as long as thou
canst.' In other words, he recommended a step by step process of
development, of growing out of the 'sword habit'

The option of 'growing out of viewing' has been chosen by many
people. The initial glamour of the television wears off, the activities
return and the set is soon forgotten.

In any case, the number of viewing hours tends to decline after the
age of twelve, (by which time the greatest damage to the child has
already been done), because teenagers become more busy with sport,
clubs, boyfriends, girlfriends, training and examination work.

There are various ways of 'growing out of viewing' for families.
Parents may actively encourage all kinds of hobbies, sport, outings,
reading stories together, singing, gardening, and visiting friends.
Conversation and meal times are cultivated, as are holidays through
which the whole family comes together on a deeper level. Young

children become the means to exploring the neighbourhood socially, through playgroups and nursery schools for example. (We have made many valued friends through our children). There are common family activities like gardening or working on the allotment. Special visits to the cinema to watch good films may be appropriate.

Even in areas where there are few play facilities, housing such as tower blocks which are inherently unsuited for young children, or no garden space — some limited alternative activities to viewing may be possible. The fact that city planners, architects and housing officials allow the construction of buildings which are highly inappropriate for children shows how limited many people's awareness of what families' and children's life needs are. This is where television becomes a community problem, for it is society which decides whether there will be enough nursery schools, playgroups, housing fit for children and play facilities, for example. My experience of tower blocks is not great and I would therefore prefer not to say much concerning what to do about television in such conditions. Perhaps the provision of nursery schools, playgroups, toy libraries, adventure playgrounds, social facilities or such campaigns as 'Mum, talk to me' might be of limited help. I appreciate that for many concerned readers 'what to do about children in tower blocks' may be the most urgent question. This book's main focus, however, is on the majority of children who live in more decent conditions but who, whatever socio-economic background they come from, watch television a great deal.

One most effective alternative to television, especially for T.V. addicted children with their short attention spans, is live puppet shows. I have several friends who go around church halls, playgroups, schools, children's parties and people's flats, giving puppet shows using Grimm's fairy tales, African and Indian folk tales. The response is tremendous, even from the teenagers who sheepishly bring younger brothers and sisters. One puppeteer, Gisela Bittleston, who taught me how to perform simple shows, started her work deliberately as an alternative to viewing. Her book is a wonderful introduction to the art of puppetry.[4] I have found that primary-aged children usually love to make, present and watch puppet shows, and it is a good family activity.

The aim of this fourth option — to grow out of viewing — may take a few weeks or months to accomplish. Whilst for a family's younger children, viewing may be severely restricted or even banned, (as smoking or drinking are) even though family life has become much more active, the television set may still be available in the home. After a certain age, children may want to watch special programmes like *Blue Peter*, and learn discrimination in their choice of programme – that is when they have the time to watch.

Many people wrote in, mentioning peer group pressure on their children to watch, and that for this reason alone they would not totally like to abandon the set. Others mentioned that children from families with no television, and who also were *not* encouraged to engage in positive alternative activities, were more susceptible to becoming tele-addicts at their friends' houses. One person mentioned that strict viewing rules in later childhood and early adolescence might also result in excessive viewing during later teenage years.

'The four week programme', 'growing out of television' and 'the limited viewing with clear rules' options may each be linked with the making television a conscious decision strategy.

## Making television a conscious decision

Children often watch television because they are bored. Instead of experiencing their boredom as a springboard for new or different activities which will come to them after working through their bored state – it is all too easy to switch on television. A particularly vulnerable time is just after school, when children could be doing a regular household task, looking after pets, playing outside or being with friends.

A major aid to making the decision to watch television a conscious one is to put it out of sight. The set need not be put in the most obvious place in the sitting room, but in a cupboard, or covered up with a cloth. Some sets are even in special cupboards with closing doors. The set can be put in a colder, more uncomfortable room, where people have to be quite motivated by the programme content to watch at all. The set could be put in a place from which it has to be removed and plugged in before watching – moreover , there should be only one set in the house.

For many children, 'out of sight' is 'out of mind' – they may forget about the television set even when they are bored. Making viewing conditions relatively uncomfortable forces a conscious decision to view a specific programme. The bother of carrying a set and plugging it in may act as a barrier to automatic viewing.

Another way to make viewing a conscious decision is not to have the most up to date set, to make viewing less attractive and to remind viewers that it is after all an 'artificial' medium. A concert pianist I once met recommended less than perfect record players for a similar reason – to remind listeners that live sound was different from reproduced sound. A video may also be used as an aid to conscious viewing with older children and teenagers, of special programmes or films, for example. However uncontrolled videos can be greatly abused with the viewing of 'adult films', often without parental knowledge. Some families I know therefore keep the video in a locked cupboard. Others prefer not to have one at all. The fashion for showing videos at children's parties will be short lived, it is hoped, as the usual party games are more fun.

The five options – the four step method, getting rid of television altogether, of limited viewing with strict rules, of growing out of television and of making television watching into a conscious choice, need to be discussed thoroughly by the parents. One option, a combination, or a new alternative then needs to be chosen. It can help to decide on a timescale for the experiment, say a month or two, and even to ask another couple to agree to help one in reviewing one's experiences. Co-operation between families can be very helpful in tackling the television question.

## Creating a lively family culture.

Having decided on an option, the next step is to try creating a lively family culture before finally putting the option of your choice into practice. Once things are livening up, there may be less resistance to getting rid of the set, to making viewing a conscious decision, and to limiting viewing. This may happen naturally in some cases.

The experiment may need some protective conditions. Drastic steps may in a few cases be highly effective – (like a ritual smashing of the set!) – but often back-sliding takes place because nothing has been done to prepare the way for breaking the habit and replacing it. Small steps, carefully taken, reviewed and discussed between both parents may be more likely to succeed in the long run.

A second development condition could be timing, for example waiting for the set to break down and not replacing it, using the excuse of higher fees not to renew the licence or phasing in new activities after a summer holiday without television.

Some degree of protection is needed for a family to undertake such an experiment, especially if it is regarded as 'odd' by friends. One non-viewing parent when asked if he had seen such and such a programme, rather than admit to not having a set, merely says he has been doing something else. Once you mention you have no set in certain circles, heavy conversations about why you should have one are inevitable, in spite of the odd 'I envy you' comment. It is as strange as not smoking was fifteen years ago. Many people offer to give you an old set, because they think you are 'depriving the children. Nobody seems interested in giving us washing machines, chairs or a fridge,' said one parent.

An important aid in giving up television for one schoolteacher's family was having like-minded neighbours, which was a big help. He wrote: —

> Since my family were forced (by wife and self) to give up T.V. altogether, they seem to have settled down to life without it very happily. It's true that my eleven year old son, when he's bored, does complain that he can't watch T.V.; but when he had it he watched and complained of being bored! Now he makes models, rides his bike, paints, tears about with the tele-free next door neighbours' children, plays the cornet in the local silver band and reads all the rest of the time, when not quarrelling with his sister. .

This teacher observed that when they had television, 'they couldn't turn the damn thing off, even when, by their own admission, they wanted to and despised what they were watching'. He and his wife took the opportunity of moving house — fortunately near to tele-free neighbours — to curtail their set rental.

Experimenting with small steps aimed at creating a more lively family culture, even if it is only reading a bedtime story, or having meals without the television set on, or instituting regular outings on Sundays instead of viewing — will hopefully build up more confidence in one's ability to handle the problem. Often this is helped by feeling one is not alone, that others are trying similar experiments, and that a growing body of professionals concerned with child development believe that trying alternative activities is better for children than just viewing. (Even the BBC T.V. ran a programme entitled, *Why don't*

*You Just Switch Off Your Television and Go and Do Something Less Boring Instead*).

Many families who had eventually given up television, or which had never had one, were very grateful for the increased confidence the original *Television and Child Development* leaflet gave them. A mother of two wrote how relieved she was, to read in the 'Guardian' about the T.V. Action Group: —

> We have not got a television, and have never had one... Our children aged between one and seven show no inclination of wanting or needing a set. We are the only parents in our area who think like this, and our neighbours and friends think us odd. . . Therefore, we find it most encouraging that our views are shared.

The helpful conditions of like-minded friends and neighbours, somewhat protected conditions, taking small steps, choosing the right time for major steps such as removing the set, and above all first developing a livelier family culture — will lead to many experiences, successes and failures. As previously mentioned, it might be important to review these thoroughly, perhaps with friends, before finally deciding on taking one option and clear plan of action. Up until now, you have been feeling your way, trying things out and have laid down the right conditions for breaking your television habit. With the groundwork well prepared, the final choice of your option for dealing with television should have a successful outcome. The challenge of meeting the television question creatively may be the occasion for exploring an exciting new family life-style.

## Childen playing at friends' houses : other families

A difficult problem is how to bring up the subject of television when one's children play at their friends' houses. One parent found that her twelve year old son had watched *Police Academy 5* at a friend's house. The friend had a T.V. and video in his bedroom, and the parents neither knew they were watching, nor did they know that their son ever had this particular video. He had taped it himself.

In this case, after discussing what had happened, the parent mentioned that she would prefer that her son did not watch whilst visiting. Perhaps being open and clear is the best way, but it is hard to be tactful, especially when one wants to maintain good relationships and not appear odd. No doubt, this is a good issue for assertiveness training to tackle!

However, there is no substitute for talking things through with one's children. In any case, if one's children like playing and know how to occupy themselves, they choose like minded friends and avoid the occasional "heavy viewer" child who is so difficult to "keep entertained".

Best of all is to develop a network of like minded families, which can share festivals, interests, outings, and children's activities. If this is matched by a school which supports such family styles with a clear lead from teachers, then the support systems can be helpful.

## *The danger of 'forbidden fruit'.*

Too many rules, rigidly applied and not enough alternative activities, may cause the "forbidden fruit" syndrome. Your children may feel deprived of television and go to watch at friends' houses instead. One group of teenagers I know from a 'T.V. teetotal' family, repaired an old set, fixed up an electricity supply, and enjoyed their viewing happily ensconced in an isolated hut in a wood. It took a year for their parents to find out.

Our older children can at least say they have a T.V. set at home, even if they rarely watch it. Very occasionally they watch a programme just to find out what a soap like *Neighbours,* or *Eastenders* is about. However, their friends are not that much interested in T.V. except the occasional special interest programme. We are surprised at how little they watch, how much they use what they watch, and the fact that they are so fully occupied there are no need for 'T.V. rules'.

## *What can schools do?*

The attitude of a school towards television may have considerable influence on parents and pupils, particularly at the nursery and infant levels. An infants school, by merely having a television set in each classroom, may legitimate the medium as 'educational' in the eyes of parents. One such school I visited used television as an aid to teach children to read, for example.

If a school is concerned about television watching levels amongst its young children, one option is to initiate such schemes as toy and book libraries, parent afternoons and home visits as vehicles for helping parents understand how to meet the all–round educational needs of their children. Some nursery schools see their roles in educating parents and children as equally important at this stage, but the former role is far from easy. One teacher commented how hesitant she is to introduce the television subject with parents, because it might 'ruin an otherwise good relationship'. In one school, a practical list of activities for children of each group was discussed with and sent round to parents – it was entitled 'What to do instead of watching T.V.'.

Many non-television parents mentioned how often teachers in primary schools used certain programmes for homework, or for classroom discussions, thereby bringing pressure to bear on their children. It is to be hoped that teachers will become sensitive to this problem when they are more informed about the effects of the medium. Indeed, school television programmes may well come to be used more sparingly and thoroughly, since the harmful effects of the medium will need to be balanced by the learning from the programme content.

Most schools do not have a clear policy on their approach to television, and if parents or teachers request one, this could be a fruitful opportunity for discussing the effects of the medium. Certainly, the T.V. Action Group's leaflet was used by P.T.A.'s and staff groups all up and down the country for this purpose. Even Shirley Williams, a former Minister for Education, has set a precedent when she expressed concern about pupils' long viewing hours. Tactful letters to parents expressing a school's views on this subject might be helpful.

Ron Jarman, a teacher, who worked in a Steiner school which had a policy which discouraged viewing for children up to the age of twelve, described concretely how they tackled the problem:–

There is only one effective way of discouraging T.V. viewing. This is by having meetings of parents of the single class, describing viewing's effects, which parents can observe in their children anyway, and stimulating the mutual support needed to first limit viewing and then stop it altogether. General parent meetings for the whole school are of little value, for most parents lack the courage to exert their authority over their children. They need the moral support of those adults they are closest to.

Only in those schools which have regular meetings for the parents of a class — in which all aspects of school life and child development are discussed — will this mutual support arise. Class meetings called solely to discuss the T.V. problem may be a waste of time. Successful meetings I have attended have always included at least one parent declaring that he has actually got rid of his set.

Schools should be seriously worried about the television question, after all, many pupils spend more time watching than they are in class. One secondary teacher found that his third year, lower stream pupils watched on average twenty-five to thirty hours a week — they were also barely literate and never read fiction. Those with high score watching time on T.V. had very low scores on reading time.

In his letter this teacher expressed little hope of persuading his head to circulate a letter to parents about the dangers of excessive T.V. viewing because, 'As he has just raised £3,000 for a new video and colour T.V. for the school, I have doubts if he'll be very keen. Anyway, he's the sort of man who doesn't persuade parents; he orders them'.

Teachers can also initiate projects aimed at a deeper understanding of the medium, and a critical awareness of programme content. A visit to a television studio with senior pupils may be highly instructive to see the 'reality' behind the screen, and how programmes are made. Making a video film may be a useful activity. At secondary level, awareness of the nature of the television medium may be cultivated through comparing it with the other media. (I have met 'media studies' students who are quite shocked by the ideas of Neil Postman or Jerry Mander — it is often the first time they have been challenged to look closely at the medium). Important questions many teachers of English already tackle are the values, ideas and assumptions underlying advertising, the news and the choice of programming by the television companies. It is to be hoped that such school activities will arouse a detached interest in the strengths and weaknesses of the medium, that will enable pupils to make more conscious choices about viewing.

The foregoing suggestions may go against the grain for some critics of television such as Jerry Mander who believe the medium to be irredeemable since it is almost impossible to view it as a normal object in a detached way. Some people exploring the matter in depth may come to similar conclusions. Meanwhile, it is evident that used indiscriminately it works against the healthy development of the child and for this reason alone, thinking parents and adults might see that 'childhood' is protected from such harmful effects.

A parent reported having attended a P.T.A. 'Television for Schools' meeting recently, where two speakers from the West Midlands Arts attempted to promote 'a more critical awareness' of television in the schools. He wrote that: —

> I kept quiet while the speakers hanged themselves by admitting that even if children were to become more critical, the BBC and IBA were impervious to criticism and that future channels would be run by purely commercial interests equally impervious. What then, was the point of wasting school time and public money in attempting to teach discrimination of a medium whose character they admitted would in fact never alter? . . . They had no answer. (The meeting was not well attended. Apparently there was a good film on that night).

Finally, some brave teachers have even tried experiments with classes encouraging them to try 'life without television' for a period. For example a Florida school teacher, Kathy Flores, suggested that both she and a class of young teenagers tried to stop watching for two weeks. She herself did more than she believed possible in that time — vowing never to return to her old television habits. The results were startling. Homework improved, conversation was rediscovered, pupils slept better and were more attentive in class. Family projects were started and some pupils volunteered to do more housework. On parent commented that, 'From now on, we will regard the television set as we do prescription medicine — to be used cautiously, and with some degree of intelligence.'[6]

Some schools have a clear policy of "no television" for nursery, kindergarten and infants classes. These include the Waldorf or Steiner schools which aim to give a creative, all-round education. They also encourage families to limit television by means of alternative activities. As one teacher said to a parent concerned about their child's viewing, "You'll soon find that she becomes so lively, active, full of fun and interests, that T.V. will be forgotten."

# Chapter Ten

## *The Emperor and the Nightingale*

'We're so pretty, you're so pretty — pretty vacant' is a line, no doubt sung with tongue in cheek, from a punk rock song. Is a whole generation of children being rendered 'pretty vacant' by viewing television as much as or more than they are in school? Indeed, is the medium itself pretty vacant?

The Australian psychologists Fred and Merrelyn Emery suggest that television is indeed a vacuous medium in their recent article, *The Vacuous Vision — the T.V. Medium*. They ask, 'What actually happens when a person sits down and looks at a functioning television screen?' What does the act of viewing do to viewers?[1] One basic point the Emerys put forward about watching television is that a person 'is looking at a radiant light signal constantly changing at either fifty or sixty half-frames per second. We suggest that the human perceptual system never evolved to deal with this sort of sensory input'.[2]

The rapid electronic rate of the illumination of myriads of dots on the screen forces the brain to almost shut down, to habituate to a repetitive light source, as if registering a blank visual field. As the Emerys put it bluntly, after their detailed technical arguments, 'Telly turns you off'.[3]

The television medium, regardless of content, tends to put viewers into a state of being dominated by the non-verbal 'right hemisphere'; viewers tend to react to the medium, as opposed to the content; it is difficult to reflect, or to be conscious of one's awareness whilst viewing: heavy television results in similar states to those produced in sensory deprivation experiments; viewing tends to release the old brain and the neural areas connected with emotional life, from control by higher neural centres, with such consequences as impulsive behaviour after viewing.

The basic argument of this book is that the act of television viewing is detrimental to child development. It affects the senses, the brain, motor skills, language, imagination and thought. The act of viewing may be far more harmful, particularly for young children who are inherently sensitive to their surroundings, than any beneficial content which is seen.

Furthermore, by perpetuating the idea that disadvantaged children may learn from television, the achievement gap is being widened. Advantaged children may also not develop their fullest possible potential — for television is a 'look and forget medium'.

By the time many children reach nursery school, the damage caused by excessive viewing has already been done, for pre-school children are both the most vulnerable to television watching's negative effects, and probably the heaviest viewers.

Viewing constitutes a 'great time robbery' for young children, since for them their play is their work. Television has caused the loss of many real life play and learning opportunities.

Although the process of viewing may be consciously mastered by adults and teenagers, some of whom are able to distance themselves from television, to control their use of it, by virtue of a more complete state of sensory and neurological development — childen are highly vulnerable. Their perceptual and sensory systems are still unfinished.

When young children are viewing, they are not asking questions, exploring, playing, solving problems, speaking, relating to other children, creating, using all the senses, thinking sequentially, scanning, initiating activities. Such features are typical of "learning disabled children", of whom there are a growing number.

The Australian Senate Standing Committee on Education and the Arts investigated the effects of television on child development in 1978, and said of the Emerys' theory: —

If this hypothesis were to be substantiated empirically, then it would help to explain many of the phenomena described by witnesses in relation to the effects of television on the development and learning behaviour of children. For example, if the medium has the effect of inducing a state of passivity or mental torpor in a child which can last for some hours after viewing, then this would explain the lack of concentration and creativity that many teachers have observed in their pupils in the classroom.[4]

The question of the effects of the television medium, regardless of content, is a new one in this country. Gwen Dunn, in the conclusion of *The Box in the Corner* — an excellent study of the effects of the content of pre-school television programmes on the under fives — asked such a question: —

First, we must know why John sits in front of television, whether his passivity is damaging to physical and mental development, whether it is negatively damaging because, whilst John is viewing, he does not shout or run or make any visible effort, whether such passivity establishes a habit and whether long periods of passivity alternated with periods of restless exciteability when there is no television to watch. The passivity is fact, at least among the children I saw.[5]

## Giving up and keeping going.

For families which decide to give up, watch less, or which monitor and control television, it is often helpful to list both the work involved and the benefits.

There will be extra parenting — the house will be "messier" with projects, toys and animals, the children will be more active — local libraries, nature reserves, etc., will need visiting, some money may be involved for materials, sports, outings, there may be more noise.

However, consider the benefits. There are less demanding children who are able to occupy themselves, one ceases having to be an entertainer, one can share interests, attention spans lengthen, and there are leisurely meals and conversations. Parenting becomes more work, but more fulfilling.

Keeping going may need some attention. The "T.V. Rules" may need discussion and revision. You need to decide if viewing for infants and preschoolers is healthy or not. Some "No — T.V." families keep a set specially for the baby sitter, who would not come otherwise. Festival times can be special periods for being and doing things together without the television. There are many books and activities to keep the family going during winter school holidays and rainy days.

The parents, particularly Dad, may be the real telly addicts. However, playing sports with one's children is more fun than watching most things except special events like the Cup Final. Compare the information content of half an hour's T.V. news with five minutes radio news and ask yourself which programme informs you better? How suitable is the 'News' for young children? Watch only when the children are in bed?

## Positive uses?

This book has painted a bleak picture of the effects of television on young children's development. The positive ones of television for teenagers and adults, for entertainment and education have not been discussed. The field of media studies is concerned with this area, and in any case is beyond the scope of this book.

Britain prides itself on *hitherto* having "the least worst television service in the world". In fact *Action for Children's Television* would like to see a similar approach in the U.S.A.

People often point to all the good children's programmes, Bob Geldof's use of T.V. to raise money for Ethiopia, documentaries, as a positive aspect of television content. Maire Messenger Davies, in her recent book *Television is Good for your kids* argues sensibly for many of the positive aspects of television. But there is a defensive tone, because so many people in different fields are coming to realise that television is clearly *not* good for their young children. The cover of her book shows a 9 month old baby holding a bear and a book discarded, sitting close to a live T.V. set and pointing. Two other infants are sitting close up paying divided attention, whilst another child is pointing out things on the screen to the baby.

It is understandable that creative people, dedicated to producing good television programmes for children, should feel threatened by the thesis that the television experience is 'pretty vacant'. For example the concern, warmth and attention to detail with which Biddy Baxter produced BBC T.V.'s *Blue Peter* are truly wonderful. She aimed her programme at a multi-age and non-captive audience. Individual files are kept on each child who writes to the programme. Two thirds of the items stem from viewers' suggestions, and this makes for a living contract with the eight to nine million viewers. Since it is a magazine programme, children need only view the items they like. *Blue Peter's* appeal raised over three and a half million pounds for Cambodia.

But unfortunately minimising the ill-effects of viewing on child development by strictly limiting older children's viewing to such programmes as *Blue Peter* only happens in a small minority of families. Many toddlers learn advertising jingles as opposed to nursery rhymes, numerous children stay up late and prefer adult programmes. This is not to mention the effects of viewing per se.

The question of the effects of viewing on child development is a highly unpopular one. It questions the huge vested interests of the television companies, which have an estimated total turnover of around £2,000 millions per annum. On one estimate about £3,000 millions alone is tied up in television sets in Britain. Television is the delivery system for advertising, for bringing up new consumers, and children are habituated to viewing under the thin veneer of television's educational value.

But then it can be argued that television, and the huge amounts of time devoted to viewing, is a symptom of a whole consumer, spectator culture that needs a vacuous medium to fill up time. As a drug to be administered to children, it performs similar functions to gin or opium in bygone times. In such anti-child and family conditions as tower blocks, television helps 'people adjust their minds, even though there's a fault in reality'.

Viewing may well be a symptom, but it is an important symptom that needs facing squarely. The real challenge may be one of 'growing out' of viewing through the encouragement of the development of a child and family centred society which values conviviality, creative activities and a supportive community. The television question may be seen positively as a vehicle for raising consciousness about the complex developmental needs of children.

According to Margaret Mead, the anthropologist and student of growing up in exotic societies, we live at a turning point in cultural evolution when a fundamental change has taken place in how young people 'come of age'. She describes first tribal societies, in which young people were educated and socialized into a cultural world which was conceived of as unchanging. The future mirrored the present and the past within the rhythms of time. Secondly, in such 'great civilisations' as Greece, Rome or even Victorian Britain, the young were brought up into a changing world — but it was change within 'the system' on the basis of established, shared values, traditions and customs.[7]

Finally, in our time and especially since Hiroshima, she believed that as the old cultural and social landmarks broke down, the future was opening up as a freedom space in which an increasing number of people are becoming cultural and social pioneers on a new frontier. The future is to be created and is different in kind, not just in degree, from the present. The foundation for this new stage in cultural development has been laid by our highly productive economy, which has liberated amounts of leisure time and extra surplus resources on a scale unparalleled in history.

Pioneering the cultural and social frontier calls for individual effort and initiative, to make experiments, to make mistakes, to learn from mistakes and to take limited steps. We are seeing an upsurge of all kinds of social action groups, playgroups, voluntary initiatives and varied community projects on the local level. People may look back on this time, for example at the numerous and excellent children's books that are being written or the explosion of local drama groups — as a highly creative time. Families too are beginning to explore new possibilities such as work sharing, mutual self-help, co-operative food buying, celebrating festivals or welcoming in adults or children in need of care — as ways of developing beyond the exacting phase of the 'nuclear family'.

However, what is a freedom space for some may be a vacuum for others. I can vividly remember working as a teenager in one lively area of Newcastle upon Tyne called Byker. Re-development has now removed some old pubs, shops, small factories, meeting places and terrace houses, many people have been forced to move out, thus breaking down old neighbourhood and family relationships. In spite of efforts to re-develop with care, old Byker has been undermined. Similarly, I once visited an industrial town in South Wales on a community development project where there were streets full of empty houses, with the whole community dispersed by compulsory purchase order around the city.

Into the social and cultural vacuum created by rapid mobility, by comprehensive re-development, by unemployment, by increased leisure and by the break-up of family and neighbourhood relationships, television can act as a time-filler, as a substitute — for a time. The city in which I live, for example, is probably not unusual in having a proportion of older teenagers with 'little to do', who are bored by viewing as a substitute for real life.

However, families are still the main setting in which young children are brought up. Whether parents choose to use a greater or lesser amount of television to bring up their children, seems to depend on how socially and culturally alive their families are. The more lively the family, the less television will be watched and vice versa. (Whatever economic bracket, with the exception of 'hard core' deprivation and poverty.)

Let us hope then, that as the complex developmental needs of young children and how viewing affects them are understood more widely by parents, their exposure to television will decrease. There may come a time when it is considered as damaging for young children to watch television, as it is for them to have a bad diet, to drink alcohol or to smoke.

Finally, since argument, facts, surveys and judgements tend to lose their impact after a time, a summary of Hans Christian Andersen's 'The Emperor and the Nightingale' will conclude this book. I believe his genius was able to foresee through this profound story some of the problems posed by advancing technology to human growth:—

Once upon a time there lived a nightingale in the depths of the Chinese Emperor's gardens close to the sea. Fishermen and travellers would exclaim, 'Oh how beautiful!' on hearing the bird sing in the night. When the emperor heard travellers praise the nightingale's singing above all else in his land, he ordered the bird to be brought to him. A poor kitchen girl was the only person in the palace who knew of the nightingale. She carried scraps every evening to her sick mother who lived by the seashore, and on returning would rest in the wood. She often heard the nightingale sing, which brought tears to her eyes, because it was just like her mother's kisses.

The nightingale was at first reluctant to come to the palace, for his song sounded best in the green wood. But when he came and sang in the palace, the emperor wept with joy and enchantment. The nightingale then lived at Court, in a cage, and was allowed out only when held by silken strings.

One day the emperor received a parcel which was labelled, 'Nightingale'. It was an artificial bird, brilliantly set with precious stones, silver and gold. On a ribbon was the message, 'The Emperor of Japan's Nightingale is poor compared to that of the Emperor of China'.

The artificial bird was much prettier than the plain nightingale and made an immediate success with its song. But the real nightingale quietly flew back to his beloved woods, leaving the Court with what they thought was the better bird.

Eventually the artificial bird broke down — it could no longer sing its only song, much to the emperor's grief. After a while, he became sad, he grew pale and cold — he was close to death. In vain, the emperor asked the artificial bird to sing but it remained silent.

However, the nightingale had heard of the emperor's illness, and came to sing a most lovely song outside the window. Slowly, the nightingale's song drove death from the emperor's heart. The emperor was moved by the nightingale's faithfulness and asked what reward the bird desired. The nightingale replied: —

'You have rewarded me! I shall never forget the tears in your eyes when I first sang to you. Those were the precious jewels that give joy to a singer's heart. But you must sleep now, become strong once more and I shall sing again.'

So the nightingale sang the emperor to sleep, he sang whilst the emperor was sleeping, and was singing still when he awoke. He promised the nightingale that he could sing when he pleased, and that he would destroy the artificial bird. But the nightingale replied: —

'Keep it, it only did its best. Let me come when I feel like it and of an evening I will sing for you from the tree branch by your window, for then you will be joyful and pensive. I will sing of happiness and suffering, of the good and evil that sleep around you. I must fly afar to the fisherman, to the villagers and poor peasants to sing to them also. I love your heart more than your crown — I will come and sing to you.'[8]

With that, the nightingale flew off, leaving the emperor refreshed and full of hope in life.

It is surprising to me that television has managed to last so long. As more families break the television habit, the medium will come to be used with more conscious knowledge of its side effects. Perhaps television will come to be used more carefully. Above all, perhaps the viewing habit will come to be regarded as harmful to young children as other drugs.

# References

*Introductory References — concerning television*

1.  Quoted in Marie Winn, *The Plug-In-Drug*, Bantam Books 1977 p.121 — from Professor Urie Bronfenbrenner, *Who Cares for America's Children* an address given to the Conference of the National Association for the Education of Young Children, 1970.
2.  Jerry Mander, *Four Arguments for the Elimination of Television*, William Morrow & Co. Inc. New York, p.168.
3.  Quote from a London teacher's letter to the T.V. Action Group.
4.  Fred and Merrelyn Emery, *A Choice of Futures: to Enlighten or Inform*, Australian National University, 1975.
5.  Dr. Adrian Rogers, *Television Stupor*, Pulse, 25 Aug 1979.
6.  Quoted by *Marie Winn*, ibid, p.245.
7.  A Bristol mother in a personal interview.
8.  Bruno Bettelheim, article *Nurturing the Secret Garden*, in the *Daily Telegraph* 8.8.87.
9.  E.B.White, from *Removal in Town, Harper's Magazine* October 1938
10.  Jim Trelease, *The Read-Aloud Handbook*, Penguin 1984.
11.  Neil Postman, *The Disappearance of Childhood*, Delacorte Press New York, 1982 p.153.
12.  Martin Large
13.  David Pearl, *National Institute of Mental Health*,
14.  Dr. Maire Messenger Davis, *Television is Good for your Kids*, Hilary Shipman 1989.
15.  Quoted in T.E.S. 26.11.82, article by Jane Last, *Legacy of Indifference*


*Foreword*

1.  Cedric Cullingford, *Children and Television*, Gower, 1984. Material from articles by Peter Wilby, *Why Pupils take in Little from T.V.*, Sunday Times, 13.5.84 and Jane Last, *Legacy of Indifference*, in the *Times Educational Supplement* 26.11.82.
2.  Michael Ende, *The Grey Gentlemen*, Burke, London 1974 p86.

## Chapter One

1.  *Children see too much T.V.*, article in *Daily Telegraph*, 6.9.1979 by Robin Stringer. Also see *Woman's Hour*, 21.9.1979
2.  *Britain a nation of watchers, not doers* article by Dr Devlin *The Citizen* 4.7.78, reviewing *Your Good Health*, BMA.
3.  See Peter Simple, *Daily Telegraph*, 17.10.1979
4.  *Children & Television: A National Survey Among 7—17 Year Olds* conducted by Carrick James Marsh, Market Research for Pye Limited, Cambridge 1978 see p.1 synopsis.
5.  Gloucester Natural Childbirth Trust Spring Newsletter 1978.
6.  Jerry Mander, *Four Arguments for the Elimination of Television*, 1978, William Morrow & Company Inc. New York. published in Britain by Harvester, April 1980. Marie Winn, *The Plug-In-Drug*, Bantam Books, 1977 New York. and Penguin books.
7.  See Anne Karpf, *The Case for Getting Rid of Television* The Times, 6.7.78.
8.  Daily Telegraph, 6.9.79., *Children See too much T.V. says BBC*, by Robin Stringer.
9.  *Woman's Hour*, Sept 21st 1979.
10. All these letters were sent to Faith Hall and/or the T.V.Action Group and are quoted from without mentioning names to preserve confidentiality. Future quotes from such letters will be either dated, or not referenced at all.
11. Letter from 6th Formers at Evesham County Secondary School, 14.5.79.
12. Tannis Macbeth Williams, *The Impact of Television*, Orlando, Florida, Academic Press. 1986

## Chapter Two

1.  See Marshall McLuhan, *Understanding Media*, Penguin.
2.  Marie Winn, *The Plug-In Drug*, Chapter 1. Penguin[1]
3.  *Annual Review of BBC Research Findings* No. 14 1988 p163.
4.  Edward de Bono, *Future Positive*, Maurice Temple Smith Ltd 1979 p146.
5.  Joan Anderson Wilkins, *Breaking the T.V. Habit*, Scribers 1982 p12.
6.  Personal interview with author.

7. Personal interview with author Observations by Robert Mehta, November 1979.
8. Jerry Mander, ibid, p159.
9. See Marie Winn, ibid, p23—33.

## Chapter Three

1. Tony Schwartz, *The Responsive Chord*, Garden City, New York, Anchor Books, 1973.
2. Peter & Iona Opie, *Language and Lore of School Children*, Oxford.
3. Quoted in Rahima Baldwin, *You are your child's first teacher*, Celestial Arts, Berkeley, 1989, p36. From Burton White, *The First Three Years of Life*, Prentice Hall, New York p19.
4. Fred & Merrelyn Emery, *A Choice of Futures — To Enlighten or Inform* No. ACP 2600,1975 Centre for Continuing Education, Australia National University, Canberra.
5. See *New Internationalist* Jan 1983 p24—25 article on *Long Distance Hypnosis*.
6. Joyce Nelson, *The Perfect Machine : TV in the Nuclear Age*, Between the lines, Toronto 1987.
7. Joyce Nelson, ibid p69.
8. *New Internationalist*, ibid, p25.
9. Joyce Nelson, ibid p70. See also H. Krugman, *Electroencephalographic Aspects of Low Involvement Implications for the McLuhan Hypothesis*, 1970 American Association for Public Opinion Research.
10. Joyce Nelson, ibid, p73.
11. Jerry Mander, *Four Arguments for the Elimination of Television*, William Morrow & Co Ltd, New York p274.
12. Jerry Mander, ibid p303.
13. Joyce Nelson, ibid, p109.
14. Joyce Nelson, ibid p108.
15. This is quoted in Rose K. Goldsen, *The Show & Tell Machine*, Dell Inc, Delta Book, 1978 p241.
16. Quoted in Marie Winn, ibid, p62—3.

## Chapter Four

1. Dr. F. Leboyer *Birth Without Violence*, Wildwood House 1975.
2. See R.M. Crosby, *Reading and the Dyslexic Child*, Souvenir Press.
3. Eva Frommer, *Voyage Through Childhood Into the Adult World*. Pergamon Press 1969 p23.
4. *See Eva Frommer, ibid*, p36.
5. Eva Frommer, *ibid*, p68
6. Rahima Baldwin, *You are Your Child's First Teacher*, Celestial Arts, San Francisco, 1989.

## Chapter Five

1. Fred and Merrelyn Emery, *A Choice of Futures — To Enlighten or Inform*, p86. The Emerys commented: Ninety-six hours of deprivation is a fairly lengthy experimental period and yet Krugman's subject was as seriously affected by a few minutes television as subject C was by his 96 hour experience.
2. Title taken from *The Care and Development of the Human Senses* W Aeppli, Steiner Schools Fellowship 1956.
3. See *Golden Blade*, 1975, editors Adam Bittleston and Charles Davy, article by John Davy *'On Coming to our Senses'* pp39—52 on which the preceding account is based.
4. See A. Koestler, *The Act of Creation*, p158 and p526, 1964
5. See F. & M. Emery, *A Choice of Futures* p171. Quotes from W. James (1890 p403—4). A school eye doctor connects this latter phenomenon with the increase in myopia.
6. Dr T.Stuart-Black Kelly of the Community Health Department of the Royal United Hospital at Bath writes that children's eyes need to be protected from possible television damage:—
   Short sight has recently been shown in over 90% of cases to be due to the child looking at near objects for too long a time compared with the time looking into the distance, i.e. it is self inflicted in children... Accommodation for close work by the eyes, i.e. reading, toys or close T.V., raises the pressure inside the eyes in some children. This pressure is not released as it should be by looking into the distance, because the child does not bother to do so. So the eye expands and becomes larger. The

larger eye can only focus on objects a short distance away, so the eye is now short sighted.

Dr Kelly therefore recommends a minimum amount of television watching for children, and to sit no closer than ten feet. He recommends this because many children watch whilst close to the set (like the two children in the Guardian 'Point of Viewing' article already mentioned above) and because: —

'The eye always focuses on any blurred object by accommodating until the picture is clear. If it cannot focus clearly it probably over accommodates i.e. more pressure, more myopia. In America the T.V. is very bad because most sets seem to be 24 inches, which are always less clear than the normal person at the same distance... children are probably over-accommodating to focus the blurred picture. This is made worse by coming close.'

Letter from Dr T Stuart-Black Kelly F.R.C.S.to Miss Simms, BBC T.V. 30 November 1978.

7.   F.& M. Emery, ibid, p71—72.
8.   See J.M. Heaton, *The Eye*, Tavistock, 1968.
9.   Quoted in R. Baldwin, ibid, p297.
10.  J. Mander, ibid, p209.

## Chapter Six

1.   F. Leboyer, *Birth Without Violence*, Wildwood House 1975 p16.
2.   Eurfron Gwynne Jones, *Points of Viewing*, Guardian — Nov 20th 1979.
3.   This threshold is considered safe, although radiological experts acknowledge that no level, even low levels of radiation, can be regarded as absolutely safe. Television sets now have a double screen and X-ray inhibitors. It is difficult to know if Ott's 1960s experiments would be repeatable with solid state modern sets, although it is hoped that such research will be followed up.
4.   See Jerry Mander, *ibid*, p175 for references.
5.   See Jerry Mander, *ibid*, p178. Also John N Ott, *Health & Light*, Devin Adair, Old Greenwich, Connecticut,19
6.   John N Ott, *Health & Light*, Pocket Books, New York 1976, p125—126.
7.   John N. Ott, *ibid*, p126—127.
8.   Jerry Mander, *ibid*, p179.

9.   Jerry Mander, *ibid*, p187—188.
10.  Jerry Mander, *ibid*, p180.
11.  Dr. John Ott, *Health & Light*, p140. Again such experiments need repeating, since their health implications, if true, are serious.
12.  Joyce Nelson, *The Perfect Machine*, Between the Lines, Toronto, 1987, Ch 11.
13.  Rosalie Bertell, *No Immediate Danger*, The Women's Press 1985.
     Television and Epilepsy. I have come across some interesting research on television-induced epilepsy, to which 1 in 10,000 are susceptible. See *Seizures Induced by Flickering Light'*, R.F.Hess, G.F.A. Harding and N. Drasdo, University of Aston. Vol 51 — August 1974. American Journal of Optometry & Physiological Optics. Television is a precipitant of light-induced fits — both normally functioning sets and faulty sets may act as triggers. The most vulnerable situation is when a person sits close to the set in a dimly lit room.
     *Television and Migraine*. Some people suffer from visually induced migraine, of which television can be a cause. See Debney, L.M.,Phd Thesis, 1978: *Migraine — A Study of Environmental and Intrapersonal Factors*, the University of Aston Library.

## Chapter Seven

1.   J. Trelease, *The Read-Aloud Handbook*, Penguin, London, 1984.
2.   N Postman, *Amusing Ourselves to Death*, *ibid*, p145.
3.   Quoted from a letter to the T.V.A.G. 12.5.1978.
4.   H.T. Himmelweit, A.P.Oppenheim & P. Vince *Television & the Child*, Nuffield Foundation 1958 O.U.P. London. References & quotes from T Weihs, *Television & the handicapped child*, *The Cresset*, Vol. X No. 3 Summer 1964.
5.   Quotes and references are taken from Gaynor Thomas, *Some Effects of Television on Children*, dissertation, Summer 1977 p10. See Milton Shulman, *The Ravenous Eye*.
6.   Willard Wirtz, *On Further Examination*, Report of the Advisory Panel on the Scholastic Aptitude Test Score Decline, College Entrance Exam Board, New York 1977.
7.   Dennis Herbstein, *In need of small talk*, Sunday Times 21.1.1980.
8.   John Ezard, *T.V. puts paid to the Nursery Rhyme*, Guardian 11.5.1978.

9. F. & M. Emery, ibid p82, Quotes from Krugman p11−13.
10. See News week, Feb 21 1977, *What TV Does to Kids*, by Harry F Waters.
11. See Gaynor Thomas, ibid, from Grant Noble, *Children in front of the small screen.*
12. Leifer, Collins, Gross, Taylor, Andrews and Blackmer. *Development Aspects of Variables Relevant to Observational Learning, Child Development*, 1970. Quoted in M. Winn, ibid, p40−41.
13. From *Woman's Hour*, BBC Radio 4, 25.2.1980., Report of a recent survey in the *T.V. Times*.
14. Tim Hicks, *Toys*, unpublished paper, Hearthsong, GA., USA.
15. Dr H Edelston MD DPM *Children and Television* in *Community Health* volume 9 No.4 1978 p225−226.
16. Bruno Bettelheim, *The Uses of Enchantment − the Meaning & Importance of Fairy Tales*, Peregrine Books, 1978.
17. Roy West, *Spotting the telly-addict*, the *Liverpool Echo*, *6.2.1980. p8.*
18. *See Marie Winn, ibid.*
19. *See David Elkind, The Hurried Child*, Addison Wesley 1981, p78, quoted from E.Kaye, *The ACT Guide to Children's Television*, Boston, Beacon Press 1979.
20. Quotes from Dr Thomas Weih's article, *Television & the Handicapped Child*, ibid.
21. P. Clarke, J. Lauruol, H Kofsky, *To a Different Drumbeat*, Hawthorn Press 1989.
22. G. Stewart, *Doctors declare war on child ads* Evening Standard p12 Nov 12 1978.
23. M Messenger Davis, *Television is Good for your Kids*, Hilary Shipman p192.
24. N Postman,ibid, p152.
25. C.F. *New Internationalist*, ibid.
26. J Wilkins, ibid, p36.

## Chapter Eight

1. Quoted by Dr. H . Edelston in *Children and Television*, article in Community Health, Vol 9 No 4 1978.
2. Bel Mooney, *SCOB!*, in the *Listener*, 14.6.1986.
3. F. & M.Emery, ibid, p63.

4.  Quoted in F.& M. Emery, ibid, from M. Pawley, *The Private Future*, p69.
5.  Joan Wilkins, ibid, p34.
6.  F. & M. Emery, ibid p102.
7.  F. & M. Emery, in *The Vacuous Vision — The T.V. Medium*, published in the *Journal of the University Film Association*.
8.  J. & D. Singer, article, *Some Hazards of Growing up in a Television Environment: Children's Aggression & Restlessness*, in *Television as a Social Issue* ed. S. Oskamp Sage Publications, London 1988.
9.  J. & D. Singer, ibid, p185.
10. T. Macbeth Williams, ibid Academic Press, 1986, p400−401.
11. See Nicholas Gillett, *Television, a School of Violence?*, November 1978. and see H.J. Eysenck & D.K.B. Nias, *Sex, Violence & the Media*, Temple Smith.
    For quote see N. Gillett, ibid, p2. and W.A.Belson, *Television Violence & The Adolescent Boy*, Saxon House.
12. Tannis Williams, ibid, p400.
13. See G. Cumberbatch & D Howitt, *Does television teach our children violence?*, Applied Psychology Dept, University of Aston in Birmingham No. 109.
14. See Gaynor Thomas, ibid p6−7, from Grant Noble *Children in Front of the Small Screen*, 1975. See M.J.A. Howe, *Television Children*, New University Education, London 1977.
15. Marie Winn, *Children Without Childhood*, Penguin.
16. Neil Postman, *The Disappearance of Childhood*, Delacorte Press, New York, 1982 p117.
17. Neil Postman, ibid, p153.
18. David Elkind, *The Hurried Child: Growing Up Too Fast Too Soon*, Addison Wesley 1981.

## Chapter Nine

1.  Quoted from M. Winn, *The Plug-in-Drug*, p246.
2.  See Joan Anderson Wilkins, *Breaking the T.V. Habit*, Scribners New York 1982 p53. Questions taken from and adapted from Joan Wilkins' book.
3.  Jim Trelease, *The Read Aloud Handbook*, Penguin London 1984. Chapter 7 p97.
4.  Gisela Bittlestone, *The Healing Art of Glove Puppetry*, 1978,

Floris Books.
5.  Quoted in *Light Fantastic*, article in *New Internationalist* January 1983.
6.  Hollie Herman, *Life Without T.V.*, National Enquirer 8.5.1979.
    "The consensus amongst most of the research community is that violence on television does lead to aggressive behaviour by children and teenagers who watch the programmes... in magnitude, television violence is as strongly correlated with aggressive behaviour as any other behavioural variable that has been measured." David Pearl, National Institute for Mental Health *Television & Behaviour*, Washington D.C. 1982.


## Chapter Ten

*The Emperor & the Nightingale.*
1.  F. & M. Emery, *The Vacuous Vision – The TV Medium*, Journal of the University Film Association, USA, p2. 1982.
2.  F. & M. Emery, ibid, p3.
3.  F. & M. Emery, ibid, p5.
4.  F. & M. Emery, ibid, p10.
5.  Gwen Dunn, *The Box in the Corner*, Macmillan 1977 p147.
6.  Maire Messenger Davis, ibid.
7.  Margaret Mead, *Culture & Commitment* Bodley Head 1970.
8.  See Hans Christian Anderson's *Fairy Tales*.

# Appendix I : Family Resources.

## Some Parenting Books

1. Rahima Baldwin, *You Are Your Child's First Teacher* Celestial Arts, PO box 7327 Berkeley CA.
2. Heidi Britz-Crecelius, *Children at Play : Preparation for Life*, Floris Books.
3. Diana Carey & Judy Large *Festivals, Family & Food*, Hawthorn Press.
4. Paddy Clarke, Holly Kofsky & Jenny Lauruol, *To a Different Drumbeat: A practical guide to parenting children with special needs*, Hawthorn Press.
5. Stephanie Cooper, Marye Rowling & Christine Fynes Clinton, *The Children's Year — Crafts and Clothes for Children to Make.*, Hawthorn Press.
6. Gudrun Davy & Bons Voors, *Lifeways*, Hawthorn Press
7. Joan Salter *The Incarnating Child*, Hawthorn Press
8. Betty Staley, *Between Form & Freedom*, A practical guide to the teenage years, Hawthorn Press 1989

Several of the above books, plus toys, games, dolls, instruction books, and activities for families can be obtained from Hearthsong PO Box B, Sebastopol CA 95 473.


## Some books on Television

Ben Hogan & Kate Moody, *Television Awareness Training — The viewer's guide*, Media Action, 475 Riverside Drive NY 10027.

John Fiske and John Hartley, *Reading Television*, Methuen UK 1978.

Maire Messenger Davis, *Television is Good for Your Kids*, Hilary Shipman London 1989.

Jerry Mander, *Four Arguments for the Elimination of Television*, New York, William Morrow.

Joyce Nelson, *The Perfect Machine* : *T.V. in the Nuclear Age*, Between the Lines, Toronto 1987.

Neil Postman, *Amusing Ourselves to Death*, Penguin Viking, New York 1985, *The Disappearance of Childhood*, Delacorte NY 1982.

Marie Winn, *The Plug-in-Drug*, Penguin 1984, *Unplugging the Plug-in-drug*, Penguin/Viking.

Joan Wilkins, *Breaking the TV. Habit*, Scribners, New York 1982.

Valdemar Setzer, *Computers in Education*, Floris Books, Edinburgh 1989.

# Appendix II

## "Visual Display Units: Nightmare to the Operator?"

The use of visual display units (V.D.U.'s), word processors or cathode ray tube display units is spreading rapidly. Most V.D.U.'s look like small television screens and function on the same principle.

They are used as computer terminals for such purposes as stock controls in warehouses, seat reservations, accounting systems, research, in type-setting and in telecommunications. Information is shown on the screen in words and figures, for example the current account bank statement of a customer, which has been retrieved from a central computer.

As a consequence of the 'information explosion', hundreds of thousands of programmers, typists, accounts clerks and many other people are using V.D.U.'s, often for many hours a day. In other words, in addition to the average adult viewing of television for around seventeen hours per week, many people are using television extensively at work.

For anyone interested in the effects of V.D.U.'s on health at work, the article, 'Visual Display Units: Nightmare for the Operator?' in the 20th January 1979 Ophthalmic Optician is recommended. They write that:—

"Investigations show that a number of complaints, including eyestrain, headaches and tiredness have been made, especially amongst those who are required to work in front of a display screen for long and uninterrupted periods. It is, of course, well known that any type of work which requires individuals to remain in the same position and concentrate on a specific task for long periods without a rest is likely to cause feelings of strain and tiredness, the incidence and severity of the symptoms increasing with the time spent on the task. Since the use of V.D.U.'s will continue to increase rapidly, it seems reasonable to attempt to keep such problems in their correct perspective..."

The authors then go on to attribute many of such symptoms as are mentioned above to "ocular defects, improper use and design limitations of the equipment, conditions of work, the surroundings, and psychological factors". If such care was taken with television viewing at home, as is recommended by these opticians, then perhaps some of the negative effects of viewing might be minimised.

Research shows that up to a third of employees have 'uncorrected or insufficiently corrected visual defects which affect both visual and general comfort'. Such defects can result in an overload of the visual system when concentrating for long periods. The incidence of visual fatigue caused by close work, or work requiring viewing increases with age, for people's visual performance declines from the late thirties.

Adequate background lighting is important for the use of V.D.U.'s, and some manufacturers recommended levels of lighting below the normally accepted levels. This may be harder on older people.

There should be enough space behind the V.D.U. for the operators to look around the set to a relaxing background. Interestingly, one of the authors carried out a survey on the differences between operatives using V.D.U.'s and those using other methods. They write that:—

"...It was noticeable that people who had been trained to use V.D.U.'s even after they had been using them for some years, kept their work in a very different manner to those operators still using other systems. The operators using the other systems had personalised their work with pictures and other personal possessions whilst the V.D.U area had a clinical temporary appearance and discussion with the V.D.U. operators indicated that they did not fully associate with their work or their work area even though it was their permanent position."

The authors recommend that before training for V.D.U. work, operatives should have their vision checked. Records of the ocular condition should be updated, because even though no harmful effects on eyesight from the radiation given off by V.D.U.'s or from their usage have yet been proved — such records may be helpful. If care is taken over the 'ocular stability' of V.D.U. operatives, of good design, adequate illumination and appropriate surroundings, as well as the prompt examination of complaints — many problems can be avoided.

Because of the potential health hazards to workers, the international trade union movement has studied V.D.U.'s and health intensely. One group:— particular — pregnant mothers — have gained the right in "good companies" and the civil service *not* to work with V.D.U.'s at all during pregnancy. This is because they link V.D.U. work with increased birth problems, foetal disorders and miscarriages. In spite of health physicists' assurances that V.D.U. radiation is not harmful, many working women perceive potential harm.

The *International Trade Union Guidelines on V.D.U.'s* mention unexplained incidents of reproductive problems, cataracts, and dermatitis. Much research is therefore being carried out, however:

> The approach of most manufacturers, and national occupational health boards has been to quote uncritically a small number of tests carried out on V.D.U.'s, chiefly in the United States, Canada and the U.K., and to compare these with current occupational health maximum exposure levels for each type of radiation. The results, without exception, show that the radiation for V.D.U.'s is much lower than the appropriate occupational health level, often many orders of magnitude lower. While the results of these tests provide important evidence against the existence of radiation hazards for V.D.U.'s, they do not provide proof

There are several reasons for caution: −

1.  *Not all V.D.U.'s conform to these strict standards*, − older, poorly maintained V.D.U.'s may be faulty, and imported sets may not conform to safety standards.
2.  *The occupational exposure limits may be too high*. These are set for "healthy adults", not for children or old people. "Safe" levels of exposure are being continually revised downwards, as research into low level radiation continues.
3.  *The effects of long term exposure to low levels of radiation have not been fully researched*. Therefore, total hours per day of VDU operation should be limited, even though the probability of health hazards is small. Because of the hazards associated with V.D.U. cathode ray tubes, a change to liquid crystal display is recommended.[2]

## Conclusions

Similar preventative health and viewing guidelines to the trades unions' need formulating for television use. Clearly the links between health, and the various forms of low level radiation given off by cathode ray tubes need researching. However, given the vulnerability of young children, there may be some health risks from home computer screens and from viewing television.

## References

1. Quotes taken from *The Ophthalmic Optician* January 6th 1979 pp17–18, article entitled, *Visual Display Units: Nightmare to the Operator?* by S. Rosenthal and J. Grundy.
2. *International Trade Union Guidelines on Visual Display Units.*

# Appendix III Computers

Parents always ask about computers when I give talks on television. Since home computers are used as toys by infants, this is an important question which however really merits another book. A few points only can be made.

Firstly, the computer or V.D.U. screen is a cathode ray tube – similar to a T.V. screen – with the possible health side effects which close work with a screen may have on young children. For example, quite apart from health and light, radiation emissions of a low level, the latest debate centres on the effects of low intensity electromagnetic waves on people working on V.D.U.'s.

Secondly, there is the 'hidden curriculum' of computers, i.e. the effects of the software patterns on children's mental processes. John Davy, formerly science writer of the *Observer*, considered that one result of early computer use might be to mechanise children's thinking processes at a early age. This might lead to the hindering of the development of creative, independent thinking. His article from the Columbia University's *Teacher's College Record*, editor Douglas Sloan, volume 85, no.4, Summer 1984, is reproduced below.

Thirdly, many parents are pressured by advertisements claiming how computers can help with learning and how important computer skills are to get jobs. In fact, most companies value creativity, social skills, the ability to think, alertness, the ability to learn, presence of mind and personal development – the very capacities which may be undermined by a T.V. and computer – dominated early education and childhood. Such companies claim that "state of the art" computer skills can be trained quickly, thoroughly and easily in those entering the work force. There is therefore no industrial need to give children a computing "head start".

Fourthly, there is the question of cost – home computers, software and 'pre-computers' such as 'Talking Whizz Kid' cost money. What more constructive things – paper, crayons, paint, simple games, sports items – might be more useful?

Fifthly, there is the question of the right age to introduce the computer as a learning aid, a word processor and as a tool. Valdemar Setzer, *Computers in Education*, Floris Books, Edinburgh 1989 deals with this question. One viewpoint here is to use computers in the teens when students can grasp the basics of how computers work, use computers for appropriate tasks and devise programmes.

# MINDSTORMS IN THE LAMPLIGHT
## John Davy

In this short review, I shall attempt an evaluation of Seymour Papert's *Mindstorms*,[1] and the approach to the use of computers in education it embodies.

This commentary cannot be exhaustive. The virtue of Papert's work is that it is not trivial. It impinges on fundamental questions of education, psychology, philosophy, and epistemology, and a full analysis would require a much longer treatment. My purpose here, in response to the mainly enthusiastic and uncritical reception of *Mindstorms* by teachers and parents, is to sound a sceptical note, and to justify it.

Papert's achievement is to devise a programming language, LOGO, that enables children to construct their own programs, and to control a small robot, the turtle (or an equivalent on the video screen). They can make the turtle, for example, draw shapes. The kinds of things LOGO enables children to do with turtle embody 'powerful ideas' (notably mathematical and physical ideas). Thus, says Papert, the child learns through doing, is in control all the way, has fun, and is ushered into the mathematical and computer culture with confidence. 'The new knowledge is a source of power and is experienced as such from the moment it begins to form in the child's mind' (p.21.).

Papert is not naive about the potency of the realm to which he is introducing children. Computers are tools. Tools are never neutral, but create a culture of tool users who have to operate them on the tools' terms. Computers embody a mechanised version of thinking. Will they make children think mechanically? Papert's answer is yes, they will. But LOGO enables them to *choose* to learn to think in this way. 'I have invented ways to take educational advantage of the opportunities to master the art of deliberately thinking like a computer . . . By *deliberately* learning to imitate mechanical thinking, the learner becomes able to articulate what mechanical thinking is and what it is not' (p.27).

The LOGO approach is underpinned by Piaget (with whom Papert worked for some time). But it is a 'new' Piaget, setting aside his framework of natural development in favour of a more 'interventionist' approach. In particular, it is claimed that LOGO makes it possible for children to 'concretise' formal operations well before Piaget's threshold of eleven to twelve years. Furthermore, they can enter these realms with enjoyment, and avoid creating for themselves the blocks to mathematics that easily form at this stage because formal operations seem so remote from real life. In a world shaped by the powerful ideas of mathematics, we are told, the mathematical illiteracy engendered by such blocks must be overcome, and with the help of LOGO, children may be initiated early and painlessly.

I shall question this program on three grounds: its tendency to experiential impoverishment; its uncritical 'headstart' philosophy; and its idolatry of 'powerful ideas' and computer thinking. While Papert acknowledges, briefly, that there may be situations in which thinking like a computer is *not* appropriate or useful, he claims that by deliberately learning mechanical thinking, children will become aware that this is just one 'cognitive style' and that they can choose others. He does not say what others he recognises, or how children might learn to discover, practise, and value them. He merely glances sidelong here at issues of great importance, which I shall consider briefly at the conclusion of this discussion.

Leaving aside the theoretical underpinnings, what actually happens in a LOGO learning environment? Examples are given in the book. The child sits at a keyboard with a screen, typing instructions. With the help of LOGO, the machine is programmed to draw a 'flower' (Figure 1.), then a lot of 'flowers' in a garden' (Figure 2.). Next, the child may devise a program to draw a bird (Figure 3.), then a flock of birds (Figure 4.). Then the birds can be put into motion. 'The printed page,' says Papert, 'cannot capture either the product or the process; the serendipitous discoveries, the bugs, the mathematical insights, all require movement to be appreciated' (p.93).

Now let's hold on a moment. Flowers? Birds? Movement? There is not a flower or bird in sight, only a small screen on which lines are moving, while the child sits almost motionless, pushing at the keyboard with one finger. As a learning environment, it may be mentally rich (even if the richness is rather abstract), but it is perceptually extremely impoverished. No smells or tastes, no wind or birdsong (unless the computer is programmed to produce electronic tweets), no connection with soil, water, sunlight, warmth, no real ecology (although primitive interactions with a computerised caterpillar might be arranged).

Granted, we are not discussing the teaching of botany, meteorology, or ecology, but the mastery of 'powerful ideas'. Yet the actual learning environment is almost autisic in quality, impoverished sensually,

Building Up

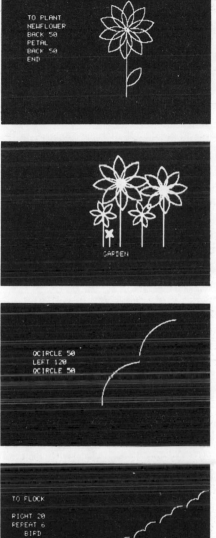

Figure 1.

Figure 2.

It's a bird

Figure 3.

Figure 4.

emotionally, and socially. (All right, children have fun, and sometimes work together on programming, a social and affective plus. But compare the scene with any traditional children's playground games, or their involvement in the ancient and wise psychodramas of fairy stories.)

In this respect, computers in classrooms are simply extensions of television in classrooms. Evidence of any profound educational value in television, except as an adjunct for good teachers (any profundity then comes from the teachers, not the television), is not known to me. It feeds us with brief stimuli and surrogate reality. All the energy that has gone into debating the effects of the content of television pro-grammes has obscured the question of sheer impoverishment of life, the effects of simply sitting for hours, absorbed in an artificial image world.

Computers, of course, are not entertainment, but LOGO makes them entertaining as a means of introducing children to powerful ideas. These are the ideas that are really shaping adult life, we are told, so why not meet them early? Put away childish things like making sand castles, feeding real turtles, playing tag in a playground rather than on a video screen and with other children rather than an electronic mouse, collecting real flowers, painting with a real brush and paints. But if you do not learn to control computers early, the earnest voices whisper, they will control you. You must give your child every chance.

If I seem intemperate, it is because of the loss of real connection with childhood of which the whole temper of *Mindstorms* is a symptom. Papert himself cannot be blamed for this. He is a brilliant exponent and champion of the dominant cultural tide, technological and instrumental in spirit and soul. When he was two, as he describes in his Foreword, Papert knew the names of lots of automobile parts, notably from the gearbox and transmission. He soon became adept at turning wheels not only in the external world but in his head (and indeed in his heart: 'I remember there was *feeling, love,* as well as understanding in my relationship with gears'). Gearwheel models later helped him into mathematics. It is fascinating glimpse into the inner life of a man with a touch of genius.

However, there really is much else in childhood besides gearwheels. No doubt young Seymour did more than turn wheels in his head. And the focus of his book has been deliberately narrowed to the question of achieving earlier, deeper, and more effective entry into some powerful ideas of mathematics. But if adopted uncritically, the message of *Mindstorms* will reinforce the tunnel vision that afflicts education, servile as it is to technocracy and easily alienated from the fullness of human experience.

Piaget, of course, made his observations and discoveries in rather richer environments (although even he had to impoverish them a little for experimental purposes). His genius was to see deeply into largely spontaneous childish operations, and to draw out of the children themselves, through conversation, a glimpse of childhood consciousness. Like many important insights, basic Piagetian realisations are often fairly obvious once articulated. The childhood skills of managing see-saws and swings are exercises in applied physics. The physics is enacted, not thought; known intuitively, not intellectually. Yet it is experience that can later be lifted into more abstract and conscious experience as a grasp of mathematical laws, calling for skills in formal operations.

The progress from sensorimotor through concrete to formal operations was regarded by Piaget as a real, natural developmental rhythm. Certainly, its unfolding calls for appropriate environmental correlates. In particular, the capacity for formal operations may scarcely develop at all if not exercised when it awakens around the age of eleven or twelve. But the idea that we are here dealing with natural developmental rhythms is challenged by Papert. As an 'interventionist', he sees Piaget's stages as capable of being concertinaed into early childhood. LOGO allows us to introduce a first practice of formal operations to seven or eight-year-olds. The computer way of thinking can thereby come 'to inhabit the young mind', providing a head start in coping with the adult world.

The results of all kind of head-start programmes should in any case lead us to be cautious in expecting clear long-term benefits from meeting LOGO at age seven. It is too early for empirical evidence to exist, so the question must be left open. But even if positive evidence did exist, it should not lead us to neglect other questions. While Piaget explored some other aspects of development and education (for example, the child's relation to moral questions), his main focus was on cognitive development. And because most educational discussion is about cognition and intellect, this is what Piaget is best known for. Since even the most goggle-eyed computerenthusiasts scarcely argue for computers as tools for affective or moral education, Piaget can be summoned to support a case that is from the beginning a kind of caricature of what education is really all about.

In *Mindstorms*, Papert tells touching stories about children intimidated by mathematics, who then learn to love learning with the help of LOGO. Their love is for the machine and the games they can play with it, echoing Papert's own infant love of gearwheels. All this would be funny if it were not so sad. It is well-known that autistic children can make close relationships with things that they cannot make with people. It could be interesting to explore whether LOGO might help some autisic children develop confidence enough to venture to play with people. But we are talking about pathologies and therapy, not education. What kind of a culture are we developing if people have to meet its most powerful ideas through machines rather than through people? If people − that is, teachers − consistently work in such a way that they block access to these ideas, should we not be looking at how teachers work rather than selling them a prosthesis? At the heart of real life is working with people, being with people, understanding people. (Does this have to be argued?) As long as classrooms include real teachers cognitive development cannot, in the nature of the situation, be divorced from emotional, social, and moral experience. Particularly in the period before puberty, while engaged in Piaget's concrete operations, children are fundamentally involved, if they are in good health, in gaining social and emotional experience. It is prime time for imaginative and artistic education. Their relationships with adults at this time influence profoundly how they relate to adults in high school including mathematics teachers. There are here very large areas of educational concern that are far more significant than demonstrating some kind of early competence in formal operations.

I should say here that I do not want to devalue computers in education altogether. That would be absurd and foolish. I take it as obvious that proper education in computer science belongs in high schools. LOGO will have real interest and value here. But there are further issues that need attention. LOGO is a sophisticated language requiring considerable computing capacity. It may help entry into powerful ideas, but is it the best way to understand computers themselves?

Much has now been written about the ease with which we project aspects of ourselves onto these machines (and indeed, we really meet aspects of ourselves, notably our own capacity to 'think like a computer', in the programs we use). The potential for obsession, delusion, and confusion is now well known, but no less a cause for concern for all that. The best medicine would surely seem to be proper insight into both the principles by which the machines operate and, still more fundamentally, the essential features of the 'style' of thinking that computers embody and demand. For this, we need 'transparent' systems, right down to the level of machine language. The force of development is to make sophisticated systems cheap enough for schools. There is little commercial incentive to sell transparent systems. But there is a significant intellectual interest and challenge. How can one open up for fifteen-year-olds the history of thought from which emerged Boolean algebra, information theory, the Turing machine? What tools would help? LOGO is, in its own terms, a brilliant achievement. But it uses this background to learn to operate within certain realms of powerful ideas. The interest in these is presented as power. The inner background, the spiritual choices that are actually being made when we think like a computer are not illuminated by playing with LOGO, since they are not grasped in any wider historical or cultural context.

Yet without concern for this context, LOGO and its like can only serve deeper idolatry of that 'instrumental reason' which Joseph Weizenbaum, in his famous and penetrating polemic,[2] rightly identifies as one of the most serious illnesses of the computer age. Despite Papert's (unsupported) claim that early thinking like a computer will promote awareness of other styles of thinking, the entire temper of his work is in the spirit of instrumental reason. This is revealed very clearly in his argument that as learners, we are all fundamentally *bricoleurs* − structuralist jargon for 'tinkerer' − assembling bits and pieces of materials and tools, which one handles and manipulates. Learning is learning to operate, to control, to be competent instrumentally. It is pragmatism in action. Truth is what can be made to work, the means are the ends. It is a tide of thought that runs so deep and strong through our technocratic society that one challenges it at one's peril. So it is worth looking at two more examples from *Mindstorms*.

To get a digital computer to draw a circle, one must break down the curve into many small straight lines. The LOGO program makes this explicit to the user. As Papert rightly says, this introduces children to the powerful idea of differentials. Essentially, this is the technique developed by Newton and Leibniz whereby continuous but variable processes can be mathematically grasped by breaking them down into infinitely small discrete steps. It is an abstract and very powerful method, a most fundamental tool in mathematics and physics. It is also a kind of essence of instrumental reason. With it, we can manipulate a biological growth curve mathematically. This can easily obscure the fact that if we 'differentiate' an actual living plant, it will not grow any more. We have killed it.

Papert gives, in another context, the example of learning to understand the flight of birds. He argues that his approach is not ordinary reductionism, because we get nowhere with the problem by studying feathers. Our grasp of bird flight came from grasping mathematical aerodynamics and by building aircraft. By analogy, Papert argues that computer systems and artificial intelligence can 'act synergistically with psychology in giving rise to a discipline of cognitive science whose principles would apply to natural and artificial intelligence'. (p.165).

This disguises the circular problem buried here. No one denies that computer systems can throw light on aspects of human intelligence. Quite obviously, the systems themselves are products of this intelligence, and so by studying them, we study aspects of ourselves. The emphasis needs to be on *aspects*. Leaving out, now, the emotional and moral questions touched on earlier, the very force and success of computer systems, and the powerful ideas of physics and mathematics, easily allow them to occupy the whole ground. We take a limited truth for the whole truth, because this particular style of thinking gives such power.

Our culture is quite extraordinary in this combination of idolatry of a particular kind of power, while floundering fundamentally in helpless anomie. A good part of the problem in my conviction, lies in the tendency of instrumental reason to prevent our asking important questions. This can be illustrated by pursuing Papert's bird flight example a little further.

While Papert sees himself drawing on the structuralist tradition, in which we owe much to Piaget, his structures are those of received mathematics (more exactly, the 'mother structures' of the Bourbaki school). There is no discussion of how complete a description of the universe might be based on these structures. They 'work' for the realms of powerful mathematical ideas with which Papert is concerned. There is a structuralist version of reductionism going on here. This is the more striking in that some biologists, also concerned with things like birds and bird flight, and realising that received Darwinism is preventing our asking a lot of rather important questions, are also looking to structuralism for new progress.

Yes, aerodynamics throws light on how bird flight is physically possible. But such insights tell us nothing about why birds fly from place to place. Aerodynamics enables us to see more deeply into the 'adaptations' of birds for flight. All living organisms are adapted in very 'intelligent' ways to their environments. We have to expend much intelligence (using a form of intelligence closely allied to instrumental reason) to understand these adaptations. Yet the concept itself is quite problematic,[3] since the the word presupposes a 'niche', a keyhole for the key. But neither can actually be meaningfully defined without the other. At the same time, our functional biological questions easily obscure nearly all recognition of the fact that we actually have no understanding of biological forms in themselves. Birds are seen as devices for flying, whales as devices for the consumption of krill, but we lose sight of the question of why birds and whales exist at all.

Goodwin, Webster, and others have recently been arguing for a structuralist theory of *biological* form.[4] Such a theory would have its own 'mother structures'. Certainly, there would have to be some relationship with the Bourbaki structures, since the universe is coherent. But the mathematics for biological forms may be very different from the mathematics for computers. There is an important frontier of modern thought here, which can be crippled if these exploratory apprehensions are seized, limited, and treated merely as tools for instrumental reason.

Computers, by their very nature, and whether operated with LOGO or otherwise, are potent training grounds for thinking about thinking in purely functional, operational, and instrumental terms. This is the explicit philosophy of what Weizenbaum calls the 'artificial intelligentsia'. Within this framework, *Mindstorms* is a powerful and significant contribution. My contention, though, is that its brilliance is the brilliance of the pool of light beneath a street lamp at night, which features in what is evidently Weizenbaum's favourite drunk joke: The drunk is searching for lost keys in the pool of light. A policeman asks him where he lost them. 'Out there', says the drunk, gesturing vaguely into the darkness. 'Then why are you looking here?' 'Because the light's better', says the drunk.

If we are scientifically honest, the real mysteries of human consciousness are still shrouded in darkness. They do not cease to exist because we learn to operate brilliantly in a confined and tightly-defined cognitive mode. Do we do our children any service by gathering them into the lamplight, and suggesting they forget the rest? The light is flat, and there is little room to move around. Compared to the mysteries of hide-and-seek among moving shadows, it is a limited world, and modern adults are not having all that much fun living in it. And suppose the real keys to our future are not in the pool of light, but somewhere out there?

Even in mathematics there are mysteries. Highlevel pure mathematicians tend to complain that the realm where new mathematics originates is obscured for most students by instrumental reason. They are taught to manipulate the tools – hardened specialised devices needed to operate at the level of definitions, axioms, notations. But their origins are more mysterious, intuitive. Mathematics used to be called 'the Queen of the Arts'. It is not the same world as that of flowers drawn step by step by an electronic turtle.

*Mindstorms* deserves every appreciation in its own terms. It is those terms I have questioned in this brief review, especially if they are treated, by implication or by default, as sufficient for education or for life. And if it seems that I am making a mountain out of a molehill – after all. *Mindstorms* is a short book, with a limited aim – it is because, if it is a molehill, it is sited on the slopes of the mountain of instrumental reason. And embedded in the issue of truth as power, or truth as wisdom, is a fundamental spiritual crisis of our time.

1984

1   Seymour Papert, *Mindstorms: Children, Computers, and Powerful Ideas* (New York: Basic Books, 1980).
2   Joseph Weizenbaum, *Computer Power and Human Reason* (San Francisco: W.H. Freeman, 1976).
3   Richard C. Lewontin, *Adaptations, Scientific American 239*, No3 (September 1978): 212–30.
4   G. Webster and B.C. Goodwin, *The Origin of Species: A Structuralist Approach, F. Social Biol. Struct 5* (1982): 15–47.

# Other books in the Lifeways Series

**THE CHILDREN'S YEAR. Crafts and clothes for children to make.**
Stephanie Cooper, Christine Fynes-Clinton and Marye Rowling.
You needn't be an experienced crafts person to create something lovely, and the illustrations make it a joy to browse through while choosing what to make first. *The Children's Year* offers handwork for all ages and individualities, it reminds us of the process of creating as opposed to merely consuming, and all this in the context of nature's rhythm through the year.

The authors are parents who have tried and tested the things to make included in *The Children's Year*, with their own families.
Paperback or hardback; full colour cover; (267mm x 216mm); 220pp; several hundred illustrations. ISBN 1 869 890 00 0

**FESTIVALS, FAMILY AND FOOD.** Diana Carey and Judy Large.
*'Packed full of ideas on things to do, food to make, songs to sing and games to play, it's an invaluable resources book designed to help you and your family celebrate the various festival days scattered round the year.'* The Observer Paperback; full colour cover; (250 x 200mm); 216pp; over 200 illustrations.
ISBN 0 950 706 23 X
Fourth impression.

**LIFEWAYS Working with family questions.**
Gudrun Davy and Bons Voors.
*Lifeways* is about children, about family life, about being a parent. But most of all it is about freedom, and how the tension between family life and personal fulfilment can be resolved.
*'These essays affirm that creating a family, even if you are a father on your own, or a working mother, can be a joyful, positive and spiritual work. The first essay is one of the wisest and most balanced discussions of women's rôles I have read.'* Fiona Handley, Church of England Newspaper.
Paperback; colour cover; 6" x 8¼" (150 x 210mm), 316pp.
ISBN 0 950 706 24 8
Third impression 1985.
Lifeways is published in German and Dutch.

**TO A DIFFERENT DRUMBEAT A practical guide to parenting children with special needs**
P. Clarke, H. Kofsky, and J. Lauruol
*If a man does not keep pace with his companions, perhaps it is because he hears a different drummer. Let him step to the music he hears, however measured or faraway.*
Henry David Thoreau.
Most of us ask instinctively at the moment of giving birth – "Is she all right?" or "Is he all there?", wanting reassurance that the newborn is a "perfect" human being. The majority of parents receive positive answers. For those who do not, a life journey to uncharted places begins. There is uncertainty,

bewilderment, or grief.

There can also be a gradual discovery of new forms of Wholeness, and the unique personality and individuality each child brings – regardless of handicap.

This is a book on practical childcare, with a difference. It is written by parents, for parents, and offers suggestions (based on experience) in such areas as sleep, feeding, incontinence, play, behaviour, growth, siblings, clothing, travel, and more. It addresses the emotional needs and development of child and adult. *To a Different Drumbeat* seeks to enhance the process of caring for children who have special needs.

In an age dominated by illusions of perfection, increasing reliance on amnio-centesis, and genetic engineering, the message here is a bold one: "Look what we can do. See how life and society are richer through diversity, and how much we can learn from our children." It is a message about growing, about loving, and about help in a specific area of parenting.

246 x 189mm; 240pp approx; sewn limp bound; colour cover; line drawings; Lifeways Series;

ISBN 1 869 890 09 4.

## BETWEEN FORM AND FREEDOM
*A practical guide to the teenage years*
### BETTY STALEY

*Between Form and Freedom* offers a wealth of insights about teenagers. There are sections on the nature of adolescence – the search for the self, the birth of intellect, the release of feeling, male female differences and character. Teenagers' growth needs are explored in relation to family, friends, school, the arts and love. Issues such as stress, depression, drugs, alcohol and eating disorders are included.

Betty Staley has taught literature and history at the Sacramento Waldorf High School for many years. She also runs workshops and serves on the faculty of the Rudolf Steiner College. She contributed to *Ariadne's Awakening*. Her three children are now grown up.

*"In this exellent book, Betty Staley has given us a compassionate, intelligent, and intuitive look into the minds of children and adolescents. Even the most casual reader of this book will never again respond to children and adolescents in the old mechanical ways... Naively, one could only wish this work were a best seller. Practically, I can only hope it will be read by a significant number of significant people – namely, parents, teachers, and, indeed, adolescents themselves."*
*JOSEPH CHILTON PEARCE author ofThe Magical Child*

If you have difficulties ordering from a bookshop, you can order direct from Hawthorn Press, Bankfield House, 13 Wallbridge, Stroud, Glos. GL5 3JA, U.K.

Telephone (0453) 757040. Fax (0453) 753295.